HEALTHY JAPANESE COOKING

NEW YORK • **WEATHERHILL** • TOKYO

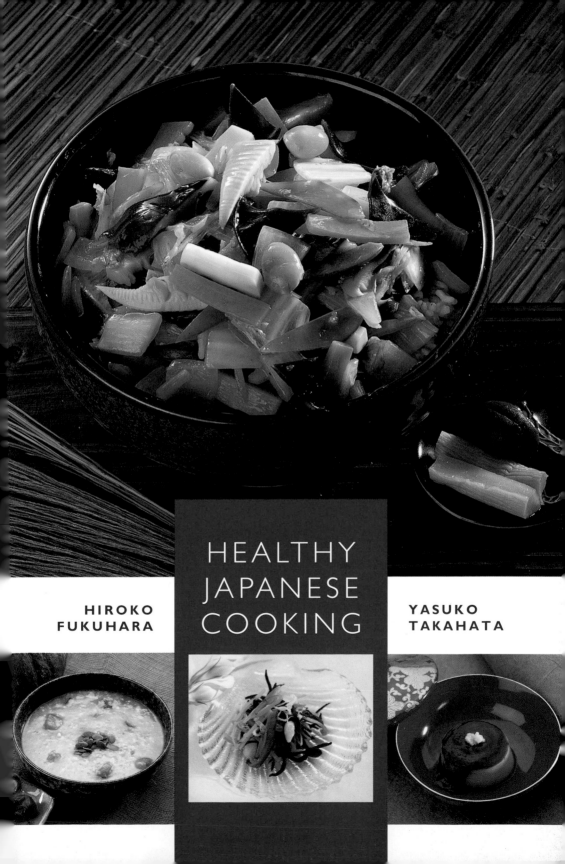

HEALTHY JAPANESE COOKING

HIROKO FUKUHARA

YASUKO TAKAHATA

The recipes and photographs in this book were originally published in two volumes of the series *Kenko Shizenshoku Ryori* (Healthy and Natural Cuisine), *Shushoku* • *Kokumotsu* (Main Dishes and Grains) and *Fukushoku* (Side Dishes), by Pegasus in Tokyo, Japan.

First edition, 1997

Published by Weatherhill, Inc.
568 Broadway, Suite 705, New York, New York 10012

Printed in Hong Kong

Library of Congress Cataloging-in-Publication Data

Fukuhara, Hiroko.
    Healthy Japanese cooking / by Hiroko Fukuhara and Yasuko Takahata.
    — 1st ed.
        p.   cm.
    ISBN 0-8348-0397-6 (soft)
    1. Cookery, Japanese.   I. Takahata, Yasuko.   II. Title
    TX724.5.J3F85   1997
    641.5952–dc21   97-27468
                                                                    CIP

CONTENTS

Introduction

MAIN DISHES

SUSHI

SIDE DISHES

INTRODUCTION

WHAT IS HEALTHY JAPANESE COOKING?

When most of us think of Japanese food, the first—and for many, the only—dishes to come to mind are the kinds of foods that Japanese people eat in restaurants or on special occasions: sushi and sashimi, with their delicate taste and appealing freshness; tempura, batter-fried pieces of shrimp, fish, and vegetables in a feather-light flour coat; and perhaps sukiyaki or shabu-shabu, thin slices of beef that the diner cooks at the table with a few twirls of the chopsticks in a pot of steaming broth. While all of these are accepted as typical Japanese foods today, by both Japanese and Westerners, in fact they are fairly recent introductions to Japanese cuisine. Sushi in its most popular form today (nigiri zushi, or hand-rolled sushi), only became popular in the early 1900s. Tempura goes back another hundred years, to the adoption of deep-fried foods from the Portuguese in the eighteenth century. And sukiyaki as we know it today is very recent, for Japanese didn't even eat beef until the 1870s, when the country began to modernize and adapt many Western ways.

The Japanese diet today is very cosmopolitan, embracing Chinese, Indian, and Southeast Asian foods just as heartily as Italian, French, American, and the ubiquitous global menu represented by the offerings of the fast food chains. It shows many of the same tendencies as the American diet toward high calorie, fat, sugar, and salt intake, though it remains, thankfully, behind the curve (or the bulge) and not as unbalanced as the former. Until relatively recently, however, Japanese food was very different, and many eating habits, customs, and tastes from earlier times survive.

Rice remains Japan's staple food of choice, though it is losing some ground to bread and pasta, and traditional Japanese cuisine was built around rice. Until about 1870, rice was not only the main crop of Japanese agriculture but the economy's main commodity. Feudal lords received their government stipends in measures of rice, and farmers paid their taxes in it, too. For the most part, only the upper classes could afford to eat rice, and when they did, they ate unmilled, or brown, rice. The common people substituted other, less expensive grains for rice, or ate a mixture of rice and other cereals, the main ones being wheat, barley, and several kinds of millet, supplemented by starchy vegetables such as potatoes and pumpkins.

Fortunately, brown rice is a very healthy, nutritionally complete food, and over the centuries the Japanese developed many delicious ways to cook it. They combined it not only with other grains but a wide variety of vegetables, flavorings, and condiments and prepared it in a variety of ways, including steaming, frying, grilling, baking, and as porridge and soup. These rice or rice-mixed-with-grain dishes are the mainstay of healthy Japanese cooking, and ideally make up more than half of a meal's volume.

In addition to main dishes, traditional Japanese cuisine included many side dishes. These consisted for the most part of leaf and root vegetables, with which Japan is richly endowed; sea vegetables, or various kinds of seaweeds; beans in many different forms, including bean-curd cake, or tofu, and fermented foods such as the bean paste known as miso and shoyu, or soy sauce; and finally, shellfish and small fishes. Over the centuries, Japanese cooks have devised many delicious and attractive ways to prepare and present these vegetables and fish. Part of mastering healthy Japanese cooking is learning those methods, as well as how to select and combine side dishes for taste and visual variety, interest, and to reflect the seasons by using the freshest ingredients.

When planning a healthy Japanese meal, start by selecting a main dish. Each of the recipes serves four, but the serving portions of the side dishes are small. The goal is to eat a variety of foods, and when selecting side dishes a good rule of thumb is one for each diner (with a minimum of two, so that even if you're eating alone you should prepare one main dish and two side dishes). Most Japanese cooks still shop every day, so they pick up whatever ingredients are fresh and delicious looking for the day's meal. Americans, with their larger and better-stocked refrigerators, tend to "shop" through that appliance's shelves, but it is important to remember that fresh foods not only taste better but are much more nutritious.

The final component of healthy Japanese cooking is seasonings, which stimulate the appetite and complement the taste of the food. Most traditional Japanese seasonings are vegetables—parsley, shiso, ginger, garlic, shallot, and so forth. Pepper and salt are also used, but sugar is conspicuously absent, mainly because it was not widely available in Japan until a hundred years ago. The absence of sugar and butter in traditional Japanese cuisine also means that Japanese desserts are quite unlike the sweet, rich desserts of Europe. Most of them are either made from lightly sweetened rice and beans or attractively but simple presented fresh fruit.

What's missing from this list of ingredients for healthy Japanese cooking? The most conspicuous absences are probably meat and dairy foods. Meat has never been eaten in Japan in the quantities it has in the West, and in fact was rarely eaten at all until Japan began to Westernize and the government actively promoted meat eating as "modern." Since cattle were scarce in Japan, dairy foods never became very popular either. As a result, the Japanese developed a cuisine that treated animal protein (in the form of shellfish and small fish) as a side, rather than a main dish, and many nutritionists today regard this as a much healthier diet altogether. This belief is supported by Japan's long life expectancy and low rates of heart disease and obesity compared to Western countries.

If you've read this far, you've realized that traditional Japanese food is not only a delicious and very attractive cuisine but a healthy way to eat, a diet that can help you lose weight and prevent disease. The next question is, what do you need to know to cook healthy Japanese food?

Healthy Japanese cooking relies very heavily on fresh, tasty, wholesome ingredients, so the first step is to learn what they are, how to find them, what substitutes can be made, and how to use them. Ingredients that may be unfamiliar to Western cooks appear in the recipes are included in the list below. The focus in the descriptions is on helping the reader recognize and find the ingredients when shopping, their use in Japanese cooking, and their nutritional properties.

BASIC INGREDIENTS

Japanese cooking uses many basic ingredients that may be unfamiliar to Western cooks, but a surprising number of them are now available in well-stocked supermarkets and health-food stores. For others, you may have to visit an Asian grocery, which have sprung up in large numbers over the last decade. It probably doesn't matter whether the Asian grocery in your area is operated by Americans of Korean, Chinese, Thai, Indian, or Japanese descent—most of the ingredients are used by more than one Asian culture.

Though the way to make the most authentic Japanese dishes is, of course, to use the ingredients Japanese cooks would, many ingredients can be substituted with no appreciable differences in the end result. For example, Japanese cooks use kuzu starch (see below) as a thickener for soups and sauces. Cornstarch works just as well, and either can be used.

Japanese vegetables present a special challenge, because they are generally smaller, have thinner skins, and are more refined in taste. Again, Asian grocery stores are an excellent source, but by carefully selecting Western vegetables one can certainly approximate the original taste in almost every case.

The most distinctive Japanese ingredients are the condiments and garnishes, and here it is worth the effort to look for the genuine article, because it is often the secret to the unique taste of a dish. There is still room for substitution, however, and suggestions are made in each recipe.

CEREALS AND CEREAL PRODUCTS

Rice

Rice has been in cultivation for at least seven thousand years. It probably originated in eastern India, though other theories suggest Thailand, Indonesia, and southwest China as the birthplace of rice. Today rice is divided into two main types, long grain and short grain rice. Rice can be grown in flooded paddies or in dry fields. It is also categorized by the nature of the exterior layer of starch into nonglutinous and glutinous rice, or "non-sticky" and "sticky" rice. Long-grain nonglutinous rice has long been cultivated and eaten in the United States and Europe. In many Asian countries, both varieties are eaten, but the Japanese only eat short-grained sticky rice. Today there are over one thousand varieties of rice grown, with many different shapes, colors, flavors, and nutritional properties, and more are being developed every day.

Brown rice is rice from which only the husk has been removed. It is alive, and will actually sprout if you plant it. White rice, on the other hand, has had the bran and the germ polished away. It is "dead rice," and will not grow if sown. Brown rice, of course, is far more nutritious and, when properly prepared, has a nutty flavor and satisfying texture that far surpasses those of white rice. As the main part of one's diet, brown rice has many advantages. It: (1) prevents and relieves constipation; (2) is extremely nutritious; (3) helps keep one mentally alert; (4) prevents high blood pressure and heart disease; (5) prevents obesity; (6) is good for stomach ailments; (7) reduces the symptoms of diabetes; and (8) is effective with infertility problems and helps prevent miscarriages.

Short-grain, sticky, white Japanese rice can be purchased at Oriental grocery stores, but we do not recommend its use. Fortunately, brown rice is much more widely available in the United States than polished Japanese rice. Most large supermarkets carry it, and all health stores stock it, usually in several varieties. Try to buy organic brown rice whenever possible. The short-grain glutinous brown rice, if available, is better tasting, chewier, and works better with the recipes in this book, but any good quality brown rice is acceptable.

Some speciality Japanese food stores may carry varieties of partially polished rice. Gobuzuki rice has half of the bran polished away, but the germ remains, and it can be seen as a golden brown point on each grain. Shichibuzuki rice has 70% of the bran polished away, and is more refined than gobuzuki. If you can find them, they are acceptable substitutes for brown rice, less nutty in flavor and faster cooking.

Rice can be mixed, before or after cooking, with other grains, as it is in many of the recipes. Cooked rice can also be fried, shaped into rice balls and grilled, or included in soups and porridges—but it always starts out steamed, and mastering the cooking of rice is the most important basic skill in Japanese cooking. Instructions for preparing rice are found in the section "Basic Recipes," below.

Millet

In Japan, millet is divided into two kinds, awa and kibi. Known in the West as foxtail millet or Italian millet, awa is an annual grain thought to have originated in the coastal regions of East Asia. The husks are shiny, and are usually yellow or white, and the seeds themselves are milky white, cream, or yellow. Like rice, there are nonglutinous and glutinous varieties. Kibi, proso millet or common millet, is thought to have originated in continental East or Central Asia. The husks may be white, gray, red, or black, and the seeds are white or yellow.

Millet is rich in protein and fat, the B vitamins, and minerals. It is also easily digestible. It is excellent at lowering blood sugar, and encourages mental alertness and general physical fitness. The nonglutinous varieties can be mixed with rice, and the glutinous varieties can be pounded together with an equal amount of rice into millet cakes. It is also milled into flour and then used to prepare dumplings and other foods, and in Asia is often an ingredient in sweets, pounded into a cake and steamed, or fermented as millet brandy. Both millet and millet flour are widely available in health-food stores.

Hatomugi

Known as Job's tears or Adlay in English, this is a grain belonging to the rice family, thought to have originated in India and Southeast Asia. In Asia it has long been used for its medicinal qualities, being effective in treating pain, urinary disorders, warts, and as a disinfectant and general tonic. It has also been used to treat neurological pain and rheumatism, and has recently been found to have tumor-fighting properties, making it useful in treating cancer. Hatomugi is an excellent skin treatment as well, recognized as effective in treating such problems as corns, blotches, eczema, rough and red skin, and bumps and swellings.

Hatomugi has a hard, luminescent husk, but is usually sold in its husked form—a pearl-shaped white grain with a white stripe. It has less sugar than many other grains and a high protein content, making it an excellent choice for diabetics and dieters. It is generally prepared by boiling it with rice, as a soup, or as a tea. Barley is an acceptable substitute for hatomugi.

POTATOES AND STARCHES

Mountain yam (yamaimo)

In addition to the potatoes (jagaimo) and sweet potatoes (Satsuma imo) that Western cooks are familiar with, the recipes in this book also use two indigenous Japanese root vegetables. The mountain yam is the rounded hairy tuber of a vine native to Japan. A cultivated form of the plant is called Yamato imo. Mountain yams consist mostly of highly digestible starch. Because they also contain amylase, polyphenolase, and oxidase, they help digest other foods eaten with them. Mountain yams have a crunchy texture and are usually prepared by grating to form a sticky paste or sauce, which ensures that the amylase functions to the fullest extent. They are best eaten raw, since the amino acids are deactivated by high cooking temperatures.

Taro

The second Japanese root vegetable is the sato imo, or taro, which is now widely available in U.S. supermarkets, since it is a staple of much Latin American and Caribbean cooking.

Konnyaku

Made from the root of a plant called variously devil's tongue or elephant foot, konnyaku is a grayish-brown jelly, very low in calories, composed of 97% water. It is eaten for its texture, which is somewhat rubbery. Since it has no flavor, it is often used in soups and stews, where it absorbs the flavor of the broth. Konnyaku is available in Japanese and Asian grocery stores in fresh, canned, and instant forms.

Kuzu starch

The kuzu plant is a vigorous vining legume. Introduced to the American south as a natural erosion control, it has created an environmental disaster, smothering and killing native plants. The tubers of the vine are used to produce a powder called kuzu starch which is used in a variety of ways in Japanese cooking, including dumplings, cakes, and noodles. It also has medicinal uses, as a nutritional supplement for children and the elderly, as a cure for diarrhea, and in the form of a traditional herbal medicine called kakkonto, which has many uses. Though kuzu starch is available in both Asian groceries and health stores, cornstarch can be substituted in recipes when kuzu is used as a thickener.

SOYBEANS AND BEAN PRODUCTS

Soybeans

Soybeans are said to have originated in north China and Siberia, but today they are grown mostly in the United States, China, and Brazil. Soybeans are often called "the meat of the fields," because they are highly nutritious, store well, and are easy to cook. As nitrogen-fixing legumes, they grow well in poor soil.

Soybeans are ubiquitous in Japanese cooking. They are eaten in their pods, boiled and salted, as a snack with beer or cold drinks in the summer.

They are simmered in a bean stew, sprinkled in powdered form over rice and rice cakes, and are the main ingredients of such basic Japanese foodstuffs as tofu, natto, miso, and soy sauce (see below). Though soybeans are rich in protein and nutrients, they are not easily digestible in whole form, but are much more so as miso and tofu (95%).

Black beans

Common in many different Asian cuisines, black beans are a variety of soy bean. Traditionally, black beans are regarded as having many medicinal properties. They are also rich in the B vitamins, iron, and calcium.

Black beans cooked with brown rice, and soy milk made from black beans are excellent for building strength and combating allergies. Boiling black beans in an iron pot, or placing an iron nail in the pot will insure that the beans have a beautiful shiny black color after cooking.

Black beans are also prepared as bean-juice miso, black bean juice, tofu, miso, soy powder, soy sauce, and bean oil, as well as eaten, boiled and salted, in the pod.

Miso (fermented salty soybean paste, with or without cereals)

Miso is categorized into three types, depending upon the type of fermenting agent used. The lightly salted white miso, and much saltier Shinshu and Sendai miso use rice as the fermenting agent. The so-called "country miso" (inaka miso) uses wheat, and hatcho miso, Nagoya miso, and tamari miso use soybeans as the fermenting agent. Miso is also categorized as sweet or salty depending upon the proportions of soybeans, fermenting agent, and salt used, and by its color. There is white miso, tan miso, and red miso. In Japan, miso is also often identified by its place of origin. Miso is judged by its luster, consistency, firmness, fragrance, and taste, in particular the latter two qualities.

Miso's distinctive smell and absorbency make it excellent for masking the odor of fish. It combines well with all kinds of meat and vegetables, and can be used in soups, stews, and grilled foods alike. To savor its distinctive fragrance, always add it last to soups and stews. Various seasoned misos, with such additions as rice vinegar, citron peel, and roasted and ground sesame seeds, are also available.

Soy sauce

Soy sauce is produced by fermenting water, salt, and a yeast made from soybeans and wheat for about one year. There are three main kinds. The saltier koikuchi soy sauce is fermented for a longer period and is thick. The less salty, or light usukuchi soy sauce is fermented for a shorter time. The variety known as tamari is sweeter than the others. Artificially brewed soy sauce, which uses amino acids and chemical processes to sidestep the natural brewing period, is now available, but it lacks the flavor, nutrition, and medicinal properties of the real thing. Soy sauce not only seasons with salt but complements and accentuates the taste of fats and oils in food. It is combined with other seasonings and flavorings to create many varieties of flavored and medicinal soy sauces.

When flavoring clear soups with soy sauce, it should be added at the last minute, so that its flavor and smell are preserved. In stews it helps prevent the ingredients from falling apart, so it should be added at the beginning, with a small amount added at the last moment as seasoning. Soy sauce is also used on grilled and braised foods, upon which it forms an appetizing deep brown glaze with a delicious aroma.

In general, salty soy sauce is used in cooking, light soy sauce is used when preserving the natural flavors and colors of the ingredients is important, and tamari is used for dipping raw fish fillets (sashimi).

Tofu
Tofu is made from soybeans that are soaked in water and then mashed into a paste-like consistency, heated, and sieved through a cloth. This liquid is coagulated with an agent called nigari, made up of magnesium chloride or calcium sulfate. Tofu is a concentrated block of high-quality vegetable protein and, in a variety of forms, plays a major part in healthy Japanese cooking. Some of the most commonly used forms of tofu are described below.

Fried tofu (abura age)
Fried tofu is prepared by slicing tofu thinly, removing the excess water, and deep-frying the slices in soy or rapeseed oil. This makes it high in fat, and when it is used as part of a stew or soup, the excess oil should be removed first by simmering the tofu slices in hot water, draining them, and patting them dry. Fried tofu also lends itself to grilling, with a miso or soy sauce and grated ginger topping. Its unique form allows it to be cut into a sort of pocket that can then be stuffed with sushi rice or vegetables.

Soy milk lees (okara)
The soy residue or lees of the tofu-production process are mostly vegetable fiber, but they can be seasoned with soup stock, soy sauce, or another flavoring and contribute fiber, texture, and water to some dishes.

Dried tofu (koridofu or koyadofu)
Dried tofu is prepared by slicing tofu, freezing it, and then drying it. It is high in fats and oils, so it spoils easily and care should be taken to ensure that it is fresh. Dried tofu can be reconstituted by soaking it in warm water, but in many recipes it is used as it is, and its spongelike texture absorbs and concentrates flavors.

Adzuki beans

These red beans are frequently used in Japanese cooking. They are rich in complex carbohydrates, B vitamins, and minerals. Unlike most beans, they are not soaked before cooking.

MUSHROOMS AND FUNGI

Enoki take

These mushrooms (Flammulina veltipes) have thin, white stems and small button tops and are grown in dense clumps. Commonly available in Japanese and Asian food stores, they have a fresh taste and a crunchy texture, and they are frequently used in soups and stews.

Kikurage

Kikurage means "tree jellyfish," and anyone who has ever savored the unique texture of jellyfish in a Chinese restaurant will recognize its similarity to the simultaneously rubbery and crunchy texture of these mushrooms. Usually sold in dried form, they are a common ingredient in Chinese cooking and widely available in Chinese food stores under the name "wood ear fungus," which is a direct translation from the Chinese. They have little taste or odor of their own, which makes them ideal for absorbing the flavors of broths, soups, and stews.

Shiitake

Shiitake mushrooms are perhaps the most widely used in Japanese cooking, and most large supermarkets in the United States now stock them both fresh and dried. Shiitake are appreciated for both their flavor and their fragrance, and have traditionally been regarded as useful in fighting colds and clearing mucous membranes. Rich in vitamin D and low in calories, they assist the body's metabolization of waste products and are effective in helping to control obesity, diabetes, and kidney disease, as well as such psychological symptoms as nervousness and apathy. Recently, shiitake have been found to contain chemicals that lower cholesterol, and they are now being analyzed for natural anticarcinogens.

Fresh shiitake are best eaten grilled and sprinkled with a little salt and then dipped in a vinegar-citrus sauce, or sauteed and served sprinkled with lemon juice. Their rich flavor is an excellent contribution to rice dishes and stews. Dried shiitake make wonderful soup stock, because their flavor is more concentrated. When reconstituting shiitake, it's important not to leave them in water too long, for they will gradually lose their flavor. It's also an excellent idea to use the water they've been soaked in as soup stock.

Shimeji

Shimeji (Lyophyllum aggregatum) are small brown button-headed mushrooms that grow in a cluster. They have a slippery texture and a nutty taste and are excellent in soups and stews. They are widely available in Japanese food stores.

Maitake

Maitake stock soup powder is sold in sealed packets in Japanese grocery stores.

NUTS AND SEEDS

Gingko nuts

Gingko nuts are available in every Chinese grocery. You can even harvest your own in the fall. They are rich in carotene, Vitamin C, calcium, and iron, and in Japan and China are regarded as a tonic that is indispensable for vitality and long life. Fresh gingko nuts, still in the shell, are prepared by parboiling and then shucking. The nut meats should then be simmered in lightly salted water for about five minutes before being mixed with rice or vegetables. Gingko nuts are also available canned, in which case cooking is unnecessary.

Lotus seeds

Lotus seeds are available in Asian groceries. Fresh lotus seeds, still green, can be eaten as they are, but the dried form is more readily available and must be boiled before eating. Several years ago archaeologists excavated a lotus seed that was 2,000 years old and germinated it. Obviously, it is a plant with a strong life force.

Sesame seeds, black & white

Sesame is a delicious and ubiquitous flavoring of Japanese cooking. Sesame-based foods, sauces, and condiments include sesame salt, parched sesame seeds, ground sesame seeds, chopped sesame seeds, sesame tofu, sesame sauce, sesame miso, sesame vinegar, sesame soy sauce, sesame dipping sauce, sesame paste, sesame sweets, and many foods deep fried in sesame oil. Rich in vitamins and minerals and attributed with a wide variety of medicinal effects, sesame is called "the wonderful herb of long life" in the East. Black sesame seeds have a stronger effect than white.

Gomashio, or sesame salt, is available already prepared in health food stores and Asian groceries, as are many other of the sesame-flavored products mentioned above.

Kukonomi

Kukonomi is a sweet-tasting bright red berry of the Chinese matrimony vine. It is sometimes available in Japanese and other Asian grocery stores, but can always be found in a Chinese herbal store, since it is widely used in East Asian cooking as a medicinal herb. The Chinese name for Kukonomi is kei chi.

Egoma oil

Egoma oil is a highly nutritious oil made from the perilla plant. In the past it was widely used in Japan as a fuel for lamps and as a waterproof coating for umbrellas and rain gear. It is a rich source of linoleic acid, which oxidizes easily, so care must be taken to make sure the oil is fresh and not to use it in too large a quantity. Safflower or peanut oil can be substituted for it.

VEGETABLES

Fern fronds (warabi & zemmai)

Warabi are the fronds of the ostrich fern and zemmai are the fronds of the royal fern, both common garden plants in North America. Fern fronds are available in fine grocery stores as well as Asian grocery stores seasonally, from spring through early summer. They have a bitter taste and must be boiled before eating. Instructions for preparing the fronds are included in the recipes that make use of them.

Mitsuba

This popular green is available in gourmet and other fine grocery stores, as well as Asian food stores. It resembles Italian parsley, which can be substituted if mitsuba is not available. Cilantro has a similar but much stronger flavor.

Garlic chives (nira)

Garlic chives are a chive with flat leaves that have a strong garlic odor and taste. They are available in Asian food stores and are wonderful in soups (they are also a major ingredient in the stuffing of the fried Chinese dumplings often called "pot stickers"). Select bunches with shorter leaves that are still tender and a dark, lustrous green.

Bamboo shoots

Bamboo shoots are available canned in most supermarkets and fresh in Asian markets. Fresh bamboo shoots should be boiled until somewhat tender but not soft. The time will depend upon their age and toughness, but they must retain their crunchy texture to be appreciated.

Sansho buds (sansho no me)

Sansho no me are the fruit of the Japanese pepper tree (Zanthoxylum piperitum). The pepper itself tastes like ordinary pepper, with a piquant twist. The buds have a much lighter taste and are widely used as a garnish. Both the fruit and the buds are usually available in Japanese food stores, and the buds are often used as a garnish on fresh fish fillets (sashimi). Any piquant herb can be substituted. Capers have a much stronger taste, because they are pickled, but can be used sparingly in the place of sansho buds.

Burdock root (gobo)

Burdock is a long, thin, fibrous light brown root that is eaten only in Japan. It has an earthy taste that comes mainly from the skin, so it should not be scrubbed too roughly before cooking. A light going over with a vegetable brush is enough. Burdock root is available in Japanese food stores, but any earthy-tasting root vegetable can be substituted for it.

Japanese radish (daikon)

Japanese radish is now widely available in the United States, and this long white root vegetable is very widely used in Japanese cuisine. It is grated to make sauces (mixed with soy sauce, for example, to dip sashimi), eaten raw, boiled, dried, and pickled. It is not nearly as hot as the red Western radish, but it still has a clear, sharp taste that complements any oily or strongly odorous foods. It also aids digestion and warms the body. When cooked, daikon absorbs other flavors and concentrates them, making it delicious in stews and soups.

Japanese turnip (kabu)

The Japanese turnip is white and rather sweetly bland. Small white Western turnips are a perfectly acceptable substitute.

Lily bulbs (yurine)

These bulbs are indigenous to Japan (also the home of the many Asiatic lilies that grace our gardens) and are occasionally available in Japanese food stores. They are very starchy, not unlike potatoes, but have a slightly sharp taste. They disintegrate rather rapidly when boiled so it is important not to over-cook them. Lily bulbs are a nice treat, but if they are not available simply increase the amount of the other root vegetables in the recipe to compensate.

Lotus root

Lotus root is actually the tuber of the lotus plant. It is crunchy, has a white skin, and can be eaten peeled or unpeeled. Lotus tuber is especially decorative when sliced, because it has a pattern of hollow areas that make each slice resemble an open flower.

Sea vegetables

Sea vegetables are widely used in Japanese cooking and a variety are available at Japanese food stores. Aonori are seaweed flakes, usually packaged in a cellophane envelope convenient for sprinkling over foods as a garnish. Hijiki is a dark brown or black algae that can be purchased in a wet pack or dried. Nori are large square sheets of seaweed, the kind used to make sushi rolls. It can be torn apart by hand or cut into strips with scissors. Instructions for toasting nori are included in the recipes that call for it. Kombu is a large kelp leaf, used in making soup stock. Japanese food stores also carry a "dried seaweed salad" in cellophane packets. It contains several varieties of dried seaweed.

CONDIMENTS AND SPICES

Sake and mirin

Both of these alcoholic beverages are distilled from rice. Ordinary sake, available at most liquor stores, is fine for cooking. Mirin is a sweet rice wine, somewhat similar to sherry. They are used in small amounts as flavorings and marinades.

Vinegars

Japanese cooking uses vinegar as a flavoring in many dishes. Always try to have rice vinegar and plum vinegar (umesu) on hand. Apple vinegar can be substituted in a pinch.

PICKLES

Pickled plums (umeboshi)

Pickled plums are a healthy snack and a wonderful way to clean the palate after eating oily or starchy foods. They are a part of every traditional Japanese lunchbox. Be careful when eating an umeboshi for the first time: the flavor is very concentrated and extremely tart. They are available in Japanese food stores.

Pickled scallions (rakkyo)

Pickled scallions are used in Japanese and Chinese cooking alike. Only the small, elongated root is pickled. The texture is crunchy and the taste somewhere between an onion and garlic. In Japan they are commonly served as a side dish with curries, and they are available in any Asian food store.

Pickled daikon

Known as Takuan after a famous monk who is credited with inventing them, these are daikon slices pickled in rice bran and salt. They are a tan to yellow color, crunchy, with a mild and somewhat musky flavor, and are available in Japanese food stores and in many health food stores.

Red pickled ginger (beni shoga)
This pickle is familiar to all who eat sushi; a small heap of sliced beni shoga is served with sushi for clearing the palate between pieces. It is available at Japanese food stores and health food stores in both sliced and whole forms.

Pickled cherry blossoms
These are sometimes available at Japanese food stores. They make a wonderful garnish for sushi. They are also easy to make, if you have a cherry tree of your own. Place 100 grams of double pink cherry blossoms (they hold up better than single blossoms) in 1 cup of red plum vinegar in a bowl with a lid that can be weighted down over the cherries. The weight should be heavy enough to keep the blossoms submerged, not to smash them. After 1 week at room temperature, drain the liquid, sprinkle the pickled blossoms with salt, and place them in a tightly sealed glass bottle to preserve them.

A delicious cherry blossom tea is made by pouring a cup of green tea over a pickled blossom or two. When using the blossoms as a garnish, rinse them quickly to remove excess salt.

Pickled shiso leaves (ume shiso)
Shiso leaves are either red or green. Red shiso is used in making pickled plums, and it gives the plums their deep red coloring. The leaves are also delicious chopped and mixed with cooked rice or sushi rice.

Kampyo
Kampyo is not a pickle but a dried vegetable. It is made from the bottle gourd, which is cut into long, thin strips and dried. Kampyo is used in sushi rolls and mixed with rice. To reconstitute the dried form, sprinkle it with salt and rub it very gently before soaking it in water.

BASIC TECHNIQUES

Most of the techniques required to make the recipes in this book are very simple and are adequately explained in the recipe sections. One area of technique, however, requires some amplification: cutting techniques.

A considerable part of the enjoyment of Japanese food comes from presentation, and presentation depends a great deal on cutting. Japanese cooks cut vegetables in ways that are intrinsically attractive, that provide visual variety, and that make the most of the particular taste and texture of the vegetable. Some of the most common cutting techniques are shown in the following chart:

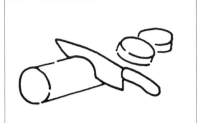

Round slices. The thickness depends upon the recipe. Used for Japanese radish, carrots, sweet potatoes, bamboo shoots, Japanese eggplants, cucumbers, lotus root, and other cylindrical vegetables. These can be trimmed with the "edging" technique described below.

Quarter slices. These are made by cutting a long, round vegetable into four quarters and then slicing them. Used for Japanese radish, turnips, carrots, potatoes, lotus roots, and other similar vegetables in stews, sauteed dishes, and soup ingredients.

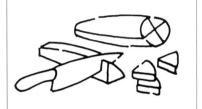

Sticks. First square the vegetable and then cut it into sticks, about 2 inches long and 3/8 inches square. Used for potatoes, Japanese radish, cucumbers, carrots, and similar vegetables when making pickles or stews.

Rough cut. Make alternate slices at opposing angles, resulting in pieces of different shape but of roughly the same size. Used for long, cylindrical vegetables such as cucumbers, Japanese eggplants, burdock, carrots, and potatoes, mostly in stews.

Wedges. First cut a round vegetable in half, and then divide that half into from two to four wedges. Used for onions, pumpkin, and squash in stews and sauteed dishes, and for other fruits and vegetables in salads and desserts.

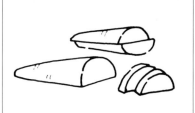

Half-moon slices. Cut round slices in half. Used for Japanese radish, carrots, lotus root, sweet potatoes, bamboo shoots, and tomatoes in stews, fried dishes, soups, and as pickles.

Matchsticks. Square the vegetable and cut into matchsticks about ¹/₄ inches on a side. Used for Japanese radish, burdock, carrots, and cucumbers in salads, simmered vegetable dishes, and soups.

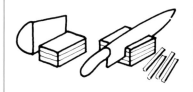

Slivers. Cut even thinner than matchsticks. Cut in the direction of the vegetable fibers to keep the vegetable from disintegrating. For Japanese radishes, carrots, cucumbers, ginger root, and onions in salads and soups.

Edging. Trim the edges of large pieces of vegetable for a beveling effect when cooking them in stews. This will preserve their shape and is very attractive. Used for Japanese radish, turnips, carrots, and potatoes.

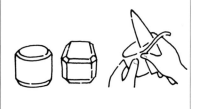

Chopping. Cut thin slices of bunches of round vegetables for garnishes or sauteed dishes. Used for spring onions, garlic chives, and cucumbers.

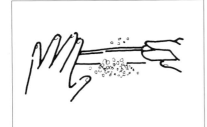

Dicing. Also used in cutting vegetables for flavoring or sauteeing, such as onions, ginger, carrots, garlic, and parsley.

Cubes. Square the vegetable and cut it into cubes about 3/8 inch on a side. Used for Japanese radish, carrots, potatoes, sweet potatoes, pumpkin, cucumbers, and tofu in salads, stews, and soups.

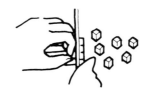

Small cubes. These should be about half the size of those described above. Used for onions, carrots, celery, and cucumbers in sauteed dishes, soups, and salads.

Footballs. Trim the edges of a the vegetable piece into the shape of a football. Used for carrots, potatoes, sweet potatoes, and other root vegetables in stews.

Angel hair. Peel a piece of vegetable about 2¹/₂ inches long as thinly as possible, and then shred very finely. Used for Japanese radish, cucumbers, and carrots as a garnish, in salads, and in stews.

SOUP STOCK

This recipe is for the basic soup stock (dashi) that is used in many recipes in this book. Stock is made twice from the same ingredients. The first stock is cooked longer and has a stronger taste. It is the one used in most recipes. The second, much lighter stock is used when it is important to preserve the delicate taste of other ingredients.

3 dried shiitake, reconstituted with water
1 4-inch square of kombu
5 cups mineral water

DIRECTIONS:

First stock (ichiban dashi)

Reconstitute the shiitake by soaking in water for about 20 minutes. Rinse the kombu and cut a fringe of 5 or 6 lines around all the edges of the square. Pour mineral water in a sauce pan and simmer the shiitake and kombu in the saucepan for 30 minutes. Remove the shiitake and kombu and save the stock

Second stock (niban dashi)

Pour 2^1/$_2$ cups of water into the saucepan and place the shiitake and kombu which were used for the first stock in it. Boil for 4 or 5 minutes, then remove the shiitake and kombu.

STEAMED BROWN RICE

Brown rice is best prepared in a pressure cooker. Not only is it far more delicious, but the resulting texture is much better. However, recent electric rice cookers with settings for cooking brown rice can also be used. When using a rice cooker, always soak the rice in the water for at least 15 minutes before starting the cooking cycle.

3 cups brown rice
3^1/$_2$ cups water
1 pinch salt
gomashio to taste

DIRECTIONS:

Rinse the brown rice and pour off the liquid. Put the brown rice and the water in a pressure cooker and let it stand overnight. Cook the rice and water over medium heat until the cooker is pressurized, then reduce the heat to low and cook an additional 20 minutes. Remove the pressure cooker from the heat and let it sit for about 10 minutes. Open the lid and mix the rice thoroughly. Serve it in rice bowls or use it in any of the main dishes calling for brown rice.

STEAMED BROWN RICE WITH MILLET

To prepare a mixture of millet and brown rice, use $1/2$ cup millet and $2 1/2$ cups of brown rice. Soak and cook the millet with the rice and follow the recipe above.

STEAMED PARTIALLY REFINED RICE WITH MILLET

Although brown rice is nutritionally superior, partially refined rice can be used if available (see the explanation of ingredients for more information about this rice).

2 cups partially refined rice
$1/3$ cup millet
$2 2/3$ cups water

DIRECTIONS:

Mix the rice and millet together, rinse it in cold water, and drain it using a strainer. Place the rice and millet mixture in a pressure cooker and add the water, mixing thoroughly. Let the mixture stand for 1 hour, then heat the pressure cooker over medium heat until it is pressurized. When the pressure cooker starts to whistle, lower the heat for 3 minutes before turning it off completely. Allow the contents to stand for an additional 10 minutes before removing the lid and mixing one more time.

SUSHI RICE

2¹/2 cups brown rice
3 cups water
I teaspoon salt
¹/4–¹/3 cup plum vinegar
3 tablespoons mirin

DIRECTIONS:

Place the rice, water, and salt in a pressure cooker. Cook in the same manner as regular brown rice, described above.

When it has finished cooking, place the steaming rice in a shallow bowl. Pour the blended vinegar mixture over it and mix it well by cutting into it with a flat wooden rice spatula. Turn over a small portion at a time, taking care not to squash the rice grains or make the rice sticky. Repeat until the vinegar is thoroughly distributed in the rice.

Fan the rice until it is cool, and then use it to prepare sushi recipes.

SUSHI RICE WITH MILLET

---

3 cups white rice
¹/3 cup millet
3¹/2 cups water
2 tablespoons sake
4 inches kombu
¹/3 cup apple cider vinegar
I tablespoon honey
I tablespoon salt

DIRECTIONS:

Wash the rice and drain it.

Soak the rice and millet in water with the sake and kombu. Cook it in the same manner as steamed partially refined rice (above), but remove the kombu before it comes to a boil.

Place steaming rice in a shallow bowl or pan. Pour the vinegar mixture over it and mix well by cutting into it with a flat wooden rice spatula. Turn over a small portion at a time, taking care not to squash the rice grains or make the rice sticky. Repeat until the vinegar is thoroughly distributed in the rice.

Fan the rice until it is cool, and then use it to prepare sushi recipes.

MAIN
DISHES

RAINBOW RICE

Orange carrot, black hijiki, yellow chrysanthemum, white lotus root, green snow peas, and the rich browns of the burdock root, shiitake, and deep-fried tofu make this a very colorful rice indeed. If chrysanthemum flowers are not available, substitute another edible flower, such as pansy, orchid, nasturtium, marigold, or hibiscus. You can also vary the recipe by substituting other vegetables, but keep both variety of color and texture in mind when making substitutions.

---

4 cups steamed brown rice with millet
1 small carrot
1/2 lotus root
soup stock (enough to cover the vegetables when cooking)
3 teaspoons soy sauce
2 teaspoons mirin
4 shiitake (reconstituted with water)
1 burdock root
1 sheet deep-fried tofu
1/4 cup dried hijiki
salt, mirin, vinegar to taste

GARNISH:
yellow chrysanthemums and snow peas for garnish

DIRECTIONS:

Soak the hijiki in water for 20 minutes and cut into 1/3-inch lengths. Soften the deep-fried tofu by pouring boiling water over it, then slice it into thin strips approximately 1/3-inch long. Set aside the hijiki and fried tofu for later use.

Slice the carrots thinly and cut them into small rectangles. Simmer them with a little salt and mirin for about 5 minutes, then set them aside.

After reconstituting the dried shiitake mushrooms in water, cut them into small squares, approximately 1/3-inch in size. (To reconstitute mushrooms, soak them in warm water for 20 minutes. Drain and squeeze excess water out with your hands before using.)

Put the burdock, fried tofu, shiitake, and hijiki in the saucepan. Add the soup stock, 3 teaspoons of soy sauce, and 2 teaspoons of mirin until the ingredients are almost covered. Cook over a low heat for 5 minutes.

Mix the cooked burdock, fried tofu, hijiki, carrots, lotus root, and shiitake with the hot steamed rice. Add a little salt to taste and serve in a bowl.

Simmer the snow peas in lightly salted water for about 2 minutes and then cut them into thin diagonal slices, as shown in the photograph. Parboil the chrysanthemum flowers in water with a splash of vinegar. Sprinkle the chrysanthemums and chopped snow peas over the rice.

Calories.............. 319
Fat...................4.3g
Carbohydrates....62.6g
Fiber...................9.8g
Sodium...............955mg

Calories...............398
Fat......................8.4g
Carbohydrates....72.0g
Fiber....................9.7g
Sodium................630mg

WINDBLOWN VEGETABLES AND RICE

This is a very attractive dish that requires a bit of dexterity to create, but it is well worth the extra effort. Decorative cutters, like cookie cutters but much smaller, can be found in Japanese grocery stores. A rustic serving dish, such as the one in the photograph, will complement this "wild" rice very nicely.

---

4 cups steamed brown rice with millet
8 chestnuts
2 pieces dried tofu
about 9 inches kampyo
1 small carrot
8 dried shiitake mushrooms
16 parboiled gingko nuts
2 tablespoons roasted white sesame seeds
10 somen noodles
soup stock
soy sauce, mirin to taste
salt, turmeric, nori, sesame oil to taste

DIRECTIONS:

Prepare the chestnuts by peeling them and cutting them into quarters. Simmer the chestnut quarters for about 15 minutes in lightly salted water with a small amount of mirin for flavoring, drain, and set them aside. Meanwhile, cut the carrot into thin slices and simmer them in lightly salted water for about 5 minutes.

Soak the shiitake in warm water for 20 minues. Drain the mushrooms and squeeze out any excess water with your hands. Save the water. Cut the shiitake into small wedges and simmer them for about 10 minutes in just enough of the water you saved to cover the pieces. Add 1 tablespoon of soy sauce and 1 teaspoon of mirin. Set aside.

Soak the dried tofu in warm water until it becomes soft. Slice it into thin strips for later decorative cutting and simmer the pieces in just enough soup stock to cover them. Add a pinch of salt, a dash of turmeric, and 1 teaspoon of mirin.

Rinse the kampyo and rub it with one tablespoon of salt. Leave the salt on for 2 minutes and then rinse the kampyo again. Next, soak the kampyo in water until it becomes soft. Cut it into short lengths and place them in a saucepan with soup stock, soy sauce, and mirin. Bring it to a boil and simmer for 8 minutes.

Chop the somen into 1-inch lengths and wrap two pieces with a bit of nori on one end to resemble pine needles, as shown in the illustration. Quickly fry these "pine needles" in the sesame oil.

Make decorative cutouts of the carrot slices, dried tofu, and kampyo. (If you don't have decorative cutters, just cut them into small squares.) Mince any small bits left over after making the decorative cuts or squares.

Now mix the hot steamed rice with the roasted sesame seeds and all of the minced ingredients. Top the mixture with the decoratively cut vegetables and tofu and the somen pine needles as if they had been tossed to the forest floor by the autumn wind.

Calories...............220
Fat.......................1.9g
Carbohydrates....44.4g
Fiber.....................2.9g
Sodium................984mg

RICE WITH DAIKON LEAVES

Daikon leaves have a distinct, slightly sharp or even hot taste. Mustard greens or broccoli rabe make excellent substitutes.

4 cups steamed rice with millet
1 handful daikon leaves
2 teaspoons salt
2 tablespoons sunflower seeds

DIRECTIONS:

Rinse the daikon leaves carefully to remove any grit and then boil them. Squeeze the boiled leaves to remove excess liquid and chop them roughly. Squeeze the chopped leaves again to remove any remaining liquid. Mix the chopped daikon leaves with salt.

Next toss the salted leaves with the hot steamed rice and millet mixture. Add more salt according to taste and garnish with the sunflower seeds. Serve hot in individual bowls.

RICE WITH UME SHISO AND NUTS

Shiso, or perilla, is now sometimes available as a garden herb. It is easier to grow than basil, to which it bears a strong resemblance, and its distinctive flavor combines well with many foods, including fresh-sliced tomatoes. It brightens up summer salads wonderfully, and combines well with vinegars. In this dish it is used as ume shiso, pickled with plum vinegar, for a tart taste treat..

---

4 cups rice with millet
2 tablespoons ume shiso
2 tablespoons pumpkin seeds
red ginger pickles

DIRECTIONS:

Squeeze the moisture out of the ume shiso and then chop it very finely. Mix the hot steamed rice with the chopped ume shiso, serve in individual rice bowls, and garnish with the pumpkin seeds and red ginger pickles.

Calories	244
Fat	4.1g
Carbohydrates	45.3g
Fiber	1.9g
Sodium	419mg

Calories...............346
Fat......................3.3g
Carbohydrates....66.9g
Fiber...................3.6g
Sodium...............945mg

RICE WITH BAMBOO SHOOTS

Cooking the bamboo shoots with the rice imparts a fresh and distinctive flavor to this dish. If sansho leaves are not available, substitute a few green peas or shredded shiso leaves.

---

2 cups brown rice
1/2 cup millet or other grain
3 cups water
4 inches soup stock kombu
1 1/2 cups chopped boiled bamboo shoots
2 teaspoons soy sauce
2 tablespoons sake
1 teaspoon salt

GARNISH:
pumpkin seeds, sansho leaves (or any green garnish such as fresh parsely,
**   snow peas, or watercress)**

DIRECTIONS:

Slice the boiled bamboo shoots thinly and then cut them into small rectangles approximately 1/4 inch by 1/2 inch. Set them aside.

Rinse the rice and millet together, and then place them in a pressure cooker. Add water and fold in the kombu, bamboo shoots, soy sauce, sake, and salt. Let the mixture stand for 1 hour. Set over medium heat until pressurized, then cook for 20 minutes over low heat. Turn off the heat and leave the mixture in the pressure cooker for an additional 20 minutes.

Transfer the mixture to a single large bowl and garnish with pumpkin seeds, sansho no me or other green garnish, and a few larger pieces of bamboo shoot, if desired. Serve immediately.

RICE WITH HEALTHY NUTS

Feel free to create variations on this recipe using other meaty nuts or seeds, making sure to prepare them so they are semi-soft in texture before you toss them with the rice. If yurine is not available, increase the chestnuts to 12.

---

2 cups brown rice
1/2 cup barley or Job's tears
4 shiitake mushrooms
3 cups water
1/2 teaspoon turmeric
1/2 teaspoon salt
1/4 cup dried yurine
1/3 cup lotus seeds (soak in water for 10 hours)
1 small carrot
1 tablespoon kukonomi
2 tablespoons pine nuts
16 gingko nuts
8 chestnuts
salt and mirin to taste

DIRECTIONS:

Soak the lotus seeds for 10 hours prior to starting this recipe.

Soak the dried shiitake mushrooms in water until soft (about 20 minutes), and then cut them into small squares, approximately 1/3 inch on a side. Rinse the rice and barley together and place the grains in a pressure cooker. Add water, turmeric, dried mushrooms, dried yurine, and salt to the rice and barley and allow the mixture to sit for about 15 minutes. Heat the pressure cooker over medium heat until pressurized, then reduce the heat to low and cook for 20 minutes. Remove it from the heat, but leave the mixture in the pressure cooker for an additional 20 minutes.

While the rice and barley mixture is cooking, peel and cut the chestnuts into quarters. Simmer the chestnut quarters in lightly salted water for about 10 minutes with a few teaspoons of mirin for taste. Drain the chestnuts and set them aside.

Dice the carrot. Simmer it in lightly salted water for about 8 minutes, drain, and set it aside. The kukonomi and gingko nuts should be parboiled briefly in separate pots, while the lotus seeds should be simmered for 15 minutes with tumeric and salt to taste.

Mix the boiled vegetables and nuts with the barley and rice from the pressure cooker in a large mixing bowl and then serve hot in individual rice bowls.

Calories...............467
Fat.....................5.2g
Carbohydrates....88.1g
Fiber...................5.3g
Sodium...............748mg

RICE WITH FRESH SOYBEANS

Fresh soybeans are a delicious source of protein, and they are nearly as good in their frozen form. If not available, try another fresh or frozen green bean or pea, but canned is not really a good substitute here. Frozen peas should be parboiled for 1 or 2 minutes in lightly salted water. The combination of the green bean and the red ginger pickles make this dish as refreshing to look at as it is delicious to eat.

---

4 cups brown rice with millet
¹/₂ cup fresh green soybeans
2 tablespoons kukonomi
2 teaspoons salt
red ginger pickles

DIRECTIONS:

   Boil the soybeans until they are soft and can be easily shelled (if using frozen soybeans, follow the instructions on the package). Salt the beans to taste. Mix the hot steamed rice with the beans, kukonomi, and two teaspoons of salt.

   Garnish with the red ginger pickles.

Calories.............249
Fat......................2.9g
Carbohydrates....46.7g
Fiber....................4.2g
Sodium...............961mg

BAKED RICE BALLS

Rice balls—onigiri—are the sandwiches of Japan, popular as lunches, picnic treats, and snacks at any time of the day. Most onigiri are made of sticky white rice wrapped in nori and formed around a core of another, complimentary treat: a pickled plum, a bit of salted fish, some hijiki, or the shiny red salmon roe called ikura. These onigiri are roasted, which brings out the nutty flavor of the brown rice.

**6 cups brown rice with millet
sesame oil
soy sauce**

DIRECTIONS:

Use ¹/₄ of the rice to make each rice ball. Wet your hands with salty water and mold the rice into a a triangular shape as shown in the photograph.

Brush the rice balls with sesame oil and soy sauce, and place them in a pan. Bake them in a preheated oven at 375 degrees for 10 minutes. The brushed rice balls can also be sauteed in a non-stick frying pan for a slightly different taste and texture.

Calories............373
Fat....................3.2g
Carbohydrates..74.4g
Fiber................5.1g
Sodium.............2109mg

VEGETABLE BURGER OVER RICE

This vegetable burger is meant to be a healthier alternative to broiled eel, a dish commonly eaten for stamina in Japan's hot, muggy summers. Instructions for scoring the patty aim to reproduce the natural texture of an eel fillet, and the sauce is a sweet barbecue sauce that eel is brushed with while it is being broiled. The scoring can, of course, be omitted. Those who aren't particularly fond of broiled eel and who like the taste of nori can vary this recipe, creating a "seaweed sandwich" by placing the vegetable burger between two sheets of nori before frying.

4 cups steamed brown rice with millet

VEGETABLE BURGER MIXTURE:
I large carrot
I lotus root
¹/4 onion
3 tablespoons kuzu starch or cornstarch
¹/2 cup whole wheat flour
I teaspoon salt
I sheet nori
sesame oil

SWEET SAUCE:
6 tablespoons soup stock
6 tablespoons soy sauce
2 tablespoons mirin

GARNISH:
chopped ginger
sansho leaves or another green garnish

DIRECTIONS:

Grate the carrot and and unpeeled lotus root together. Dice ¹/4 of an onion. Mix the kuzu starch or cornstarch with the grated carrot, lotus root, and diced onion. Add ¹/2 cup whole wheat flour to the mixture until it has the consistency of a hamburger patty. If it is too soft, add more flour.

Toast the nori by holding it over a gas or electric burner and moving it back and forth until the color darkens. (Be careful not to get it to close to an open flame, or it may ignite!) Place it on a dry cutting board and spread the vegetable burger mix on it. Cut it into 4 equal pieces. To mimic the appearance of an eel fillet, you may lightly score the vegetable burger as shown in the photograph. Fry the four "burgers" in sesame oil until dark brown.

Put the soup stock, soy sauce, and mirin in a sauce pan and simmer over medium heat for I minute to create the sweet sauce.

Serve the fried burgers on beds of hot steamed rice. Pour the sweet sauce over the vegetable burger and rice. Garnish with ginger and sansho leaves or another green garnish.

GROUND GLUTEN BURGER
AND SWEET SAUCE OVER RICE

One delicious way to eat rice is to serve it with different kinds of toppings—sauteed mixed vegetables, parboiled greens, or, in this case, a gluten-vegetable combination with a sweet sauce.

4 cups brown rice with millet

BURGER MIXTURE:
1 medium-sized ginger
4 dried shiitake mushrooms
1 cup gluten burger
4 tablespoons soy sauce
2 tablespoons mirin
2 tablespoons sake

GARNISH:
1 small carrot
8 snow peas
shredded ginger

DIRECTIONS:
   Soak the dried shiitake mushrooms in water until they become soft (about 20 minutes). Finely chop the ginger and the reconstituted shiitake mushrooms and place them in a sauce pan with the gluten burger, soy sauce, mirin, and sake. Cook the mixture over medium heat until the sauce is thickened.
   Bring the the carrot, green beans, and ginger to a boil in lightly salted water and then boil for 1 additional minute. Chop the carrots and green beans as in the illustration.
   Serve the ground gluten burger mixture on a bed of hot steamed rice. Pour the sweet sauce over the ground burger and garnish with carrot, green beans, and ginger and serve hot.

Calories.............368
Fat....................7.6g
Carbohydrates..57.6g
Fiber.................3.8g
Sodium.............1294mg

Calories............301
Fat....................5.1g
Carbohydrates..54.1g
Fiber.................3.8g
Sodium.............1102mg

SCRAMBLED TOFU OVER RICE

Scrambled tofu is a delicious alternative to eggs for the cholesterol conscious. This recipe explains how to press the excess water out of tofu, a technique commonly used in Japanese cooking when tofu is mixed with other foods to keep the dish from becoming too liquid. Feel free to experiment with other, more readily available garnishes—something tart will complement the soy, mirin, and sesame-oil flavorings perfectly—though takuan pickles, made from daikon, are certainly a delicious addition if you have them. They are a staple of the Japanese table, and so are commonly available in Japanese food stores.

---

4 cups brown rice with millet
1 1/2 blocks tofu
1 piece ginger
2 small spring onions (chopped)
1 small carrot
1 tablespoon sesame oil

SAUCE:
4 tablespoons soy sauce
3 1/2 tablespoons mirin

GARNISH:
1 sheet nori
takuan pickles
aonori

DIRECTIONS:

Place the tofu blocks on a flat surface, and then set a flat plate on top of the tofu. Place a can of soup or some other weight on the upper plate. Leave the tofu in this "press" for 10 minutes, then remove the tofu and drain off any liquid that has been pressed out. Set the tofu aside.

Mix together the soy sauce and mirin to form the sauce. Set the mixture aside.

Warm the sesame oil in a frying pan. Add the ginger, spring onions, and carrots to the pan and saute in sesame oil over medium heat for 1 minute. Scramble the tofu with a fork and add it to the frying pan. Pour the soy-mirin sauce into the pan, mixing quickly. Continue stirring gently until the mixture has thickened.

Serve the scrambled tofu over a bed of hot steamed rice. Garnish the scrambled tofu with nori, takuan, and aonori to taste.

BROWN RICE WITH KUZU SAUCE
AND VEGETABLES

2 cups brown rice with millet

I onion
$^1/_2$ carrot
2 leaves Chinese cabbage
$^1/_2$ cup chopped boiled bamboo shoots
2 Chinese wood-ear mushrooms
I small piece ginger
2 tablespoons sesame oil
4 cups soup stock
4 tablespoons kuzu starch or cornstarch
4 tablespoons water
12 parboiled gingko nuts

SAUCE:
2 tablespoons sake
2 tablespoons mirin
4 tablespoons soy sauce (usukuchi)
2 teaspoons maitake stock soup powder
2 teaspoons salt
I pinch white pepper

DIRECTIONS:
Cut all the onion, carrot, Chinese cabbage, Chinese wood-ear mushrooms, and boiled bamboo shoots into bite-size pieces. Slice the ginger into very thin strips. Create the sauce by mixing together the sake, mirin, soy sauce, shiitake soup powder, salt, and white pepper. Set the sauce aside for later.

Heat the sesame oil in a large frying pan. Add the ginger and onions first, followed by Chinese lettuce, Chinese wood-ear mushrooms, and boiled bamboo shoots, sauteeing gently over medium heat for 5 minutes. Add the soup stock and cook until the vegetables are soft.

Dissolve the kuzu starch or cornstarch in 4 tablespoons of water before using.

Slowly add the sauce to the vegetables, thickening the mixture with the kuzu starch mixture and boiled gingko nuts. Increase the heat to high for a few minutes, and add the sliced green beans just before turning off the heat.

Serve the mixture over hot steamed rice in individual rice bowls.

Calories............374
Fat....................7.6g
Carbohydrates..62.4g
Fiber..................4.0g
Sodium..............2125mg

Calories.............481
Fat......................17.6g
Carbohydrates..24.5g
Fiber...................4.8g
Sodium...............2756mg

FRIED CURRY RICE

"Curry rice" is a very popular food in Japan—so ubiquitous that some Japanese have come to think of it as "home cooking," even though of course it originated in South Asia. It is eaten in two forms, a dry curry, as in the recipe below, and a curry with sauce, as in the following recipe.

FRIED RICE:
4 bowls cold cooked brown rice with millet
2 tablespoons sesame oil
1 teaspoon salt
black pepper
$1/2$ teaspoon turmeric
1 teaspoon curry powder

VEGETABLE CURRY:
1 piece ginger
1 clove garlic
4 rakkyo (onion pickles)
1 onion
$1/2$ carrot
4 dried shiitake mushrooms
1 green pepper (or 2 small Japanese green peppers)
1 cup gluten burger
3 tablespoons raisins
1 tablespoon sesame oil
1 tablespoon curry powder
1 tablespoon salt
1 tablespoon soy sauce

GARNISH:
fresh coriander or parsley
$1/4$ apple

DIRECTIONS:

Finely chop all the vegetables, keeping each vegetable separate on the chopping board or a platter.

Heat the sesame oil with tumeric and curry powder over low heat. Add salt and black pepper to taste. Take enough cold cooked rice for four people (4 to 6 cups) and fry it in oil over medium heat. Take the fried rice out of the pan to allow the excess oil to drain off. Keep it warm.

Add more sesame oil to the frying pan and increase the heat. Add the ginger, garlic, rakkyo, onion, carrot, shiitake, green pepper, gluten burger, and raisins, in that order. Spend about 5 minutes getting all of the ingredients in, and then saute them together for another five minutes. Add more curry powder, salt, and soy sauce as needed.

Put the hot fried rice on plates. Cover the rice with the vegetable curry. Garnish with apple and parsley or coriander.

VEGETABLE CURRY OVER STEAMED RICE

4 cups brown rice with millet

SAUCE:
1 piece chopped ginger
2 cloves chopped garlic
1 chopped onion
2 cups soup stock
sesame oil

CURRY:
1 onion
1 carrot
$^1/_2$ daikon or 2 turnips
2 potatoes
2 green peppers (or 4 of the smaller Japanese green peppers)
2 tablespoons sesame oil
2 tablespoons margarine
4 tablespoons whole flour
1 teaspoon turmeric
1 tablespoon curry powder
2 cups soup stock
1 grated apple
2 tablespoons raisins
4 tablespoons chopped rakkyo (onion pickles)
2 teaspoons salt
2 tablespoons worcester sauce
2 tablespoons tomato sauce
2 teaspoons honey

DIRECTIONS:
Prepare the vegetables by chopping the onion, carrot, peppers, and daikon into small strips (approximately 1 inch in length). Cube the potatoes into small pieces. Dice the ginger and garlic. Grate the apple and chop the rakkyo into small pieces.

Prepare the sauce first. Fry the ginger, garlic and onion in a large frying pan with the sesame oil over low heat, stirring gently. Add flour, turmeric, and curry powder, continuing to saute the mixture for 1 to 2 minutes. Gradually pour 2 cups of soup stock into the pan, stirring gently. Set the pan aside, keeping it warm over low heat.

Put sesame oil in another frying pan to prepare the curry. Warm the pan gradually, sauteeing the onion, carrots, daikon, and potato for 2 to 3 minutes. Add 2 cups of soup stock and gradually mix in the grated apple, raisins, and chopped rakkyo. Cook over low heat until the vegetables are soft, about 15 minutes. Add the warm ginger-garlic sauce to the cooked vegetables. Use salt, worcester sauce, tomato sauce, and honey to season. Add the green peppers last and cook the curry for approximately 1 minute.

Serve the curry over beds of hot steamed rice on individual plates.

Calories............544
Fat....................13.6g
Carbohydrates..52.3g
Fiber.................8.1g
Sodium.............1417mg

Calories...............343
Fat.....................12.9g
Carbohydrates....48.0g
Fiber...................4.8g
Sodium...............984mg

FRIED CHINESE RICE WITH NUTS

This dish can be served attractively by pressing the rice and nuts mixture into a mold. Molds for shaping rice are available in Asian food store, but jello molds or bunt pans will do just as well.

---

4 cups brown rice with millet
1/2 onion
1/2 carrot
4 tablespoons of nuts/seeds (Choose any two of chestnuts, sunflower seeds, almonds, pine nuts, or pumpkin seeds)
2 tablespoons sesame oil
2 teaspoons salt
1/2 teaspoon pepper

GARNISH:
almonds, parsley, shiso leaf (or any green garnish that is edible raw)

DIRECTIONS:

Dice about 1 inch of carrot and 1/2 an onion and fry them in the sesame oil. Add salt and pepper to taste. Quickly mix the hot rice and millet with the fried vegetables in the frying pan. Add the nuts. Remove the fried rice from the heat and press the mixture into a cake tin or mold.

Once the rice has been shaped in the mold, turn the molded rice out onto a plate. Garnish with parsley, almonds, and shiso as shown in the picture.

RICE CASSEROLE

1 1/2 cups brown rice
1/2 cup millet
2 1/4 cups water
1/2 teaspoon salt

WHITE CREAM SAUCE:
1/2 onion
2 tablespoons safflower margarine
3 tablespoons white flour
2 cups soybean milk (unflavored)
2 teaspoons salt
pepper

GARNISH:
parsley

DIRECTIONS:

Cook the rice, millet, water, and salt in a pressure cooker over medium heat until pressurized, then turn down to low and cook for 20 minutes. After 20 minutes, turn off the heat and leave the rice in the cooker without opening the lid while preparing the sauce.

Chop the onions finely and brown them by sauteing them in the safflower margarine over low heat. Once the onions are brown, add flour and continue frying over low heat, being careful not to burn the flour or the onions. Add soy milk and gradually bring the mixture to a boil. Turn the heat to low and add salt and pepper to taste.

Put the steamed rice in an ovenproof dish. Cover the rice with the white sauce and bake it in a preheated oven for 10 minutes at 375 degrees.

Garnish with parsley just before serving.

Calories...............422
Fat.....................9.8g
Carbohydrates....68.8g
Fiber...................3.0g
Sodium...............512mg

Calories.............117
Fat.....................1.1g
Carbohydrates..25.7g
Fiber..................4.1g
Sodium..............1299mg

MUSHROOMS AND SEA VEGETABLES PORRIDGE

Packets of dried sea-vegetable salad can be purchased at Japanese or other Asian food stores. If not available, use whatever dried sea vegetables you can find there and make your own mix. You can also substitute oyster mushrooms for the enoki.

---

1 1/2 cups cooked brown rice with millet
6 cups soup stock
4 shiitake mushrooms
1 bunch enoki mushrooms
2 tablespoons sake
1/4 cup dried sea-vegetable salad (wakame, akatosaka, funori, itokanten, kukiwakame, kombu)
16 parboiled gingko nuts
4 tablespoons light soy sauce
1 teaspoon salt

GARNISH:
aonori

DIRECTIONS:
Soak the shiitake mushrooms in warm water for 20 minutes.

Soak the dried sea-vegetable salad in water to reconstitute it. Quarter the shiitake mushrooms and cut the enoki mushrooms into 1-inch lengths. Sprinkle both with sake.

Bring the soup stock to a boil and add the rice. Simmer over low heat, seasoning with soy sauce and salt when the soup is reduced by half. Add the mushrooms and simmer for another 5 minutes.

While the mushrooms are cooking, cut the sea vegetables into bite-size pieces. Put the sea vegetables and gingko nuts into the soup and bring the mixture to a boil, then remove it from the heat immediately.

Serve the hot soup in a large bowl and garnish with aonori.

PORRIDGE WITH MEDICINAL HERBS

"Medicinal herbs" (yakuzen) refers to certain herbs, fruits, and nuts that are regarded as having healing properties in Chinese medicine. Job's tears, lotus seeds, yurine, gingko, jujubes, and kukonomi all fall into this category. Prunes can be substituted for jujubes.

I cup brown rice
2 tablespoons Job's tears or barley
5 cups water
$^1/_3$ cup lotus seeds
$^1/_3$ cup dried yurine
$^1/_2$ cup jujubes or prunes
12 gingko nuts
2 teaspoons maitake soup-stock powder
I teaspoon salt
3 ounces miso
2 tablespoons sake
2 tablespoons kukonomi
2 tablespoons pine nuts
chopped chives

DIRECTIONS:

Wash the brown rice, Job's tears or barley, lotus seeds, and yurine. Put them into a pressure cooker. Add the water with a pinch of salt. Cook the mixture over medium heat until pressurized, then reduce the heat to low and cook an additional 30 minutes.

Let the mixture sit in the pressure cooker with the lid closed until the pressure dissipates, approximately 30 minutes. Lift the lid and then add the jujubes, gingko nuts, and maitake powder. Simmer for 4 or 5 minutes while stirring constantly. Season with salt, miso, and sake.

Add the kukonomi just before serving and garnish with pine nuts and chives.

Calories.............322
Fat.....................5.1g
Carbohydrates..59.6g
Fiber..................2.9g
Sodium..............945mg

PORRIDGE WITH GARLIC CHIVES

Nira, or garlic chives, resemble ordinary chives except for their thin, flat leaves that are very pungent. They are often available in Asian food stores, but chives or spring onions can be substituted. The flavor and appearance of the porridge owe at least as much to the green part of the nira as to the bulb.

---

1 1/2 cups cooked brown rice with millet
6 cups soup stock
2 tablespoons light soy sauce
2 teaspoons salt
2 tablespoons sake
1/2 bunch chopped garlic chives, chives or spring onions
2 tablespoons pumpkin seeds

DIRECTIONS:

Bring the soup stock to a boil and add the rice. Simmer them on low heat for 10 minutes. Season with sake, soy sauce, and salt, then add garlic chives.

Float pumpkin seeds on the surface of the soup and serve.

Calories.............120
Fat.....................2.8g
Carbohydrates..18.7g
Fiber..................0.9g
Sodium..............1772mg

Calories...............151
Fat.......................2.7g
Carbohydrates....27.4g
Fiber...................2.5g
Sodium...............218mg

JAPANESE PUMPKIN PORRIDGE

¹/₂ cup brown rice
¹/₄ cup barley or Job's tears, combined with millet
¹/₄ fresh pumpkin or summer squash
7 cups water
¹/₃ teaspoon salt
roasted pumpkin seeds

DIRECTIONS:

Wash the rice, Job's tears or barley, and millet, and allow the mixture to drain for 30 minutes to 1 hour. Meanwhile, remove the seeds from the pumpkin and cut the flesh into small cubes.

Place the rice, grains, pumpkin, water, and salt in a pressure cooker. Cook over medium heat until fully pressurized, then turn the heat down and cook over low heat for another 30 minutes.

Let the mixture cool in the pressure cooker for 20 minutes after turning off the heat. Season the porridge to taste with salt and garnish it with pumpkin seeds before serving.

SUSHI

MIYABI ZUSHI

"Miyabi" means elegant or refined, and this sushi, with its colorful ingredients mixed lightly together, certainly fits the bill. Serving it in a beautiful utensil, as in the photograph, will make it even more appetizing.

---

4 cups sushi rice with millet
$1/2$ joint lotus root
4 pieces dried tofu
6 shiitake (reconstituted with water)
16 inches kampyo
$1/2$ carrot
10 snow peas
2 tablespoons white sesame

SEASONINGS:
apple vinegar, honey, salt, soup stock, turmeric, mirin, soy sauce

GARNISH:
cherry blossoms pickled in salt, sansho buds, red ginger pickles

---

DIRECTIONS:

Peel and cut the lotus root into thin rings, then boil them for 5 minutes with vinegar and drain them. Mix $1/4$ cup apple vinegar, 1 tablespoon honey and $1/2$ tablespoon salt, and marinate the lotus root in it.

Soak the dried tofu in hot water until soft and then gently squeeze out the extra moisture. Simmer the reconstituted tofu with the soup stock, turmeric, mirin, and salt for 5 minutes, then cut it into interesting shapes and small pieces.

Soak the shiitake in water for about 20 minutes until soft, then drain them and save the water. Cut each mushroom into six pieces and simmer in the water that you saved, adding soy sauce and mirin for flavoring, for 5 minutes.

Wash the kampyo and then rub salt into it. Let it sit for 2 minutes, then squeeze out any excess water. Soak the kampyo in water again for 5 minutes, then simmer it with the soup stock, soy sauce, and mirin for another 5 minutes. Cut it into $1/3$-inch lengths.

Slice the carrot thinly and then cut most of the slices into decorative shapes. Dice any remaining slices. Simmer all the pieces in water with salt and mirin for 3 minutes.

Boil the snow peas in lightly salted water for 1 minute and then plunge them into cold water to cool quickly for $1/2$ to 1 minute. Cut them diagonally into pieces of equal size.

Roast the white sesame seeds and then chop them finely.

First, set aside a few of each of the ingredients above to use as a garnish, then toss the rest of each ingredient with the sushi rice. Now garnish with the reserved ingredients and cherry blossom, sansho buds, and pickled ginger. Serve in a large dish.

Calories...............392
Fat.......................10.7g
Carbohydrates....57.9g
Fiber....................6.6g
Sodium................874mg

Calories.............298
Fat.....................2.3g
Carbohydrates..61.6g
Fiber..................8.0g
Sodium.............1441mg

SUSHI SALAD WITH WILD VEGETABLES

There are many kinds of sushi, but sushi salad (chirashi zushi) and inari zushi are the most frequently made at home. Chirashi zushi consists of a variety of ingredients mixed with and also dressed over a bed of sushi rice. Though raw fish fillets and shrimp can be used, this recipe provides a variety of tastes and textures with wild vegetables. Zemmai are fern fronds, seasonally available in Japanese food stores. You can experiment with any edible wild vegetable that has a crunchy texture.

---

4 cups sushi rice with millet
$1/2$ small carrot
6 shiitake (reconstituted with water)
I cup fern fronds (zemmai)
I cup chopped boiled bamboo shoots
$1/2$ cup butterbur
I cup of salt for removing bitterness from wild vegetables
soup stock (enough to cover ingredients)
I tablespoon light soy sauce
I tablespoon mirin
I cup bean curd lees
$1/2$ teaspoon turmeric
2 tablespoons apple vinegar
I tablespoon honey
I teaspoon salt

DIRECTIONS:

Cut the carrot into thin rings and quarters. Boil in lightly salted water for 3 minutes.

Cut about half of the shiitake into $1/3$-inch pieces lengthwise and dice the rest. Boil all of the shiitake with the soup stock, soy sauce, and mirin.

To remove any bitterness, rub the zemmai fronds with $1/2$ cup of salt and then pour hot water over them and leave them until the water is cool. Rinse once more and then cut them into $1/3$-inch lengths. Boil them in soup stock, soy sauce, and mirin.

Cut the bamboo shoots into thin rings and quarters, and then boil them with soup stock, soy sauce, and mirin.

Boil the butterbur roots with salt for I minute, then peel and dice them.

Place the bean-curd lees, turmeric, apple vinegar, honey, and salt in a small pan and scramble the mixture into small pieces over low heat.

Stir the scrambled bean curd lees into the sushi rice, serve in a large dish, and garnish with the remaining ingredients.

SUSHI POCKETS

Sushi pockets are called Inari zushi after the rice god, to whom this treat is offered at little country shrines. They always consist of sushi rice mixed with other ingredients stuffed into pouches of fried tofu. Because they are so handy, they make a perfect snack or picnic treat.

---

4 cups sushi rice with millet
10 sheets fried tofu
2 cups soup stock
2 tablespoons soy sauce
2 tablespoons mirin
small amounts of the following (use to taste):
shiitake (reconstituted with water)
carrot
sesame
pine nuts
soy sauce
mirin (mix into sushi rice)
20 mitsuba
20 cherry blossoms pickled in salt

DIRECTIONS:

Cut the carrot and shiitake into pieces. Pour water over them in a saucepan until all the pieces are barely covered, then boil them with the soy sauce and mirin. Mix them into the sushi rice with the pine nuts and sesame.

Boil water in a new pan, add the fried tofu, and cook for 4 to 5 minutes. Allow the water to cool, then gently squeeze any excess water out of the tofu with your hands. Place the fried tofu back into the pan and add soup stock, 2 tablespoons of soy sauce, and 2 tablespoons of mirin. Simmer until most of the stock is absorbed by the fried tofu.

Drain and pat the fried tofu dry. Cut it in half and turn it inside out to form tofu bags. Stuff sushi rice into the bags and garnish them with mitsuba and cherry blossoms. Lotus root, burdock, snow peas, and hijiki can also be mixed into the sushi rice to create variations.

Calories...............530
Fat......................24.0g
Carbohydrates....55.0g
Fiber...................1.3g
Sodium...............792mg

Calories............423
Fat....................14.5g
Carbohydrates..59.8g
Fiber..................6.1g
Sodium..............1095mg

THREE-COLOR SUSHI POCKETS

4 cups brown sushi rice
2 tablespoons finely chopped sesame seeds
4 sheets fried tofu
Soup stock (enough to cover fried tofu)
1 tablespoon soy sauce
1 tablespoon mirin
$^1/_2$ small carrot (cut lengthwise and into strips)
10 snow peas
8 shiitake (reconstituted in water)
2 tablespoons soy sauce
2 tablespoons mirin

GARNISH:
cherry blossoms pickled in salt

DIRECTIONS:

Boil the water, add the fried tofu, and cook for 4 or 5 minutes. Drain the tofu and then simmer it with the soup stock, mirin, and 1 tablespoon of soy sauce. Mix the sesame seeds into the sushi rice.

Boil the carrot strips for 1 minute in lightly salted water.

Boil the snow peas in lightly salted water for 1 minute and then plunge them into cold water to cool. Cut them diagonally and sprinkle with salt.

Reconstitute the dried shiitake by soaking them in cold water for 20 minutes. Drain the mushrooms, but save the water. Cut the shiitake lengthwise and into strips. Put the strips in a saucepan and cover them with the water used earlier to soak the mushrooms. Simmer with 2 tablespoons of soy sauce and 2 tablespoons of mirin.

Cut the fried tofu into 2 pieces. Open the cut end to make a pocket. Stuff the sushi rice into the tofu bags and heap the other ingredients on top. Garnish with cherry blossoms.

SIDE DISHES

DAIKON TORTOISESHELLS

Tortoises are symbols of long life in Asia, and this healthy recipe featuring daikon cut in a hexagonal shape and simmered to a appetizing tortoiseshell golden brown is certain to extend your years.

---

1 daikon
4 cups soup stock
2 tablespoons sake
4 tablespoons mirin
1/2 cup soy sauce
1/4 red pepper

GARNISH:
finely chopped ginger

DIRECTIONS:
    Cut the daikon into 1-inch circular slices. Trim the slices into hexagonal shapes as shown. Simmer in soup stock, sake, and mirin. When the daikon is soft but not mushy, add soy sauce and red pepper and continue simmering until the pieces turn a deep tortoiseshell brown.
    Serve on a plate garnished with ginger.

Calories............87
Fat.....................0.1g
Carbohydrates..13.8g
Fiber..................1.4g
Sodium..............1457mg

Calories.............122
Fat....................0.6g
Carbohydrates....18.4g
Fiber..................2.2g
Sodium.............906mg

DAIKON WITH MISO TOPPING

Daikon, with its satisfying, meaty flavor, is very well complemented by miso. This is a perfect dish for a cold day.

---

¹/2 daikon
I tablespoon cake flour

BROTH:
4 tablespoons hatcho miso
4 tablespoons soup stock
4 tablespoons mirin
2 tablespoons sake

GARNISH:
grated ginger to taste

DIRECTIONS:

Cut the daikon into small slices, approximately I ¹/3 inches in width. Place the pieces into a pan, barely covering them with water. Add flour, either mixing with a small amount of water beforehand or sprinkling over the daikon pieces and stirring to avoid lumps. Simmer until the slices are soft.

While the daikon is cooking, mix together the hatcho miso, soup stock, mirin, and sake in a separate pot, bringing them to a boil.

Just before serving, spoon the soup stock mixture over the hot daikon and garnish with ginger.

CARROTS DRESSED WITH SWEET VINEGAR

2 carrots
raisins as needed
parsley to taste

DRESSING:
2 tablespoons plum vinegar
1 teaspoon egoma oil
1 teaspoon honey
dissolved mustard to taste

DIRECTIONS:
    Cut the carrots into fine strips, boil the strips for about 1 minute in lightly salted water, and then drain completely. Combine the sauce ingredients and pour it over the carrots, mixing in the raisins at the same time.
    Garnish with parsley and serve.

Calories..............45
Fat......................1.2g
Carbohydrates....7.8g
Fiber...................0.1g
Sodium...............591mg

Calories............89
Fat....................0.5g
Carbohydrates..14.6g
Fiber..................1.5g
Sodium..............1063mg

LOTUS ROOT STRINGS

1 medium lotus root
1/2 tablespoon sesame oil
1/2 cup soup stock
4 tablespoons soy sauce
2 tablespoons mirin
2 tablespoons sake

GARNISH:
poppy seeds to taste

DIRECTIONS:

Cut the unpeeled lotus root into fine strips. Mix together the soup stock, soy sauce, mirin, and sake, then set the mixture aside. Heat the sesame oil in a pan and fry the lotus-root strips, adding the soup stock and simmering for about 10 minutes until the strips are cooked and the soup stock has been absorbed or has evaporated.

Serve sprinkled with poppy seeds.

TOFU STUFFED WITH LOTUS ROOT
IN MISO BROTH

---

4 sheets deep-fried tofu
$^1/_2$ small lotus root
$^1/_3$ carrot
2 pieces dried shiitake mushroom (reconstituted with water)
I teaspoon salt
4 cups soup stock
4 tablespoons miso
I tablespoon sake
I tablespoon kuzu starch or cornstarch
I tablespoon water
8 pieces mitsuba (can substitute spinach)

GARNISH:
4 snow peas
8 flower-shaped carrot pieces

DIRECTIONS:

Put the deep-fried tofu into boiling water for 2 to 3 minutes to extract the oil, and then cut one side of each piece to make a little pouch (see photograph).

Grate the unpeeled lotus root. Cut the shiitake mushrooms and carrot into fine strips. Salt all three and stuff the mixture into the deep-fried tofu pouch. Tie the mouth of the pouch with boiled mitsuba (or spinach).

Bring the soup stock, miso, and sake to a boil, and then add the bean-curd pouch. Continue boiling for 4 to 5 minutes, adding the sake and miso. Dissolve the kuzu starch in water before using, then thicken the soup by adding the dissolved kuzu mixture.

Serve the hot soup in a bowl with boiled mitsuba. Garnish with additional carrot slices and snow peas.

Calories...............113
Fat......................3.8g
Carbohydrates....14.3g
Fiber...................2.3g
Sodium................827mg

STEAMED LOTUS ROOT WEDGES

Lotus root is available in Asian grocery stores, but pumpkin or summer squash can also be substituted in this and the following two recipes.

---

1 medium lotus root
4 dried shiitake mushrooms (reconstituted in water)
1 cup gluten burger
$^1/_2$ teaspoon salt
2 tablespoons soy sauce
poppy seeds to taste

DIRECTIONS:

Grate the unpeeled lotus root. Add minced shiitake mushroom, gluten bur-ger, salt, and soy sauce to the grated lotus root and mix together.

Put the mixture into a steamer pan and shape it into a log. Steam for 15-20 minutes over a medium flame in a steamer.

Cut into wedges and sprinkle with poppy seeds.

Calories............... 140
Fat........................ 5.5g
Carbohydrates.... 13.2g
Fiber.................... 1.7g
Sodium................ 906mg

Calories............156
Fat....................0.2g
Carbohydrates..29.9g
Fiber..................2.9g
Sodium.............1142mg

SWEET BOILED POTATOES

4 medium potatoes
1 onion
1 medium carrot
4 cups soup stock
2 tablespoons sake
3 tablespoons mirin
4 tablespoons light soy sauce
¹/3 hot pepper
2 tablespoons green peas (or other legumes)

DIRECTIONS:

Pare the potatoes and cut them into small pieces. Chop the onion and carrot, put the potatoes, carrot, and onion into the soup stock and simmer until the vegetables are soft. Season with the sake, mirin, soy sauce, and hot pepper.

Continue simmering for a few minutes, allowing the vegetables to absorb the seasonings. Add the green peas last and simmer until cooked.

Calories...............72
Fat.......................0.1g
Carbohydrates....16.1g
Fiber...................1.2g
Sodium...............394mg

POTATO AND CUCUMBER SALAD

Japanese cucumbers are much smaller and more slender than most Western varieties. They have only tiny seeds, their skins are thin, smooth, and edible, and they have a much lighter, fresher taste than other cucumbers. If they are not available, substitute a small, slender, ripe Western cucumber.

---

2 medium potatoes
1 Japanese cucumber
¹/4 carrot
1 teaspoon salt
1¹/2 tablespoons vinegar
1 teaspoon honey
pepper to taste

GARNISH:
2 tablespoons raisins

DIRECTIONS:

Steam the potatoes and mash them roughly with a fork, leaving some potato pieces.

Cut the cucumber into thin round slices and sprinkle the slices with a little salt. After a minute, squeeze them gently in your hands to remove excess water. This will cause the cucumber slices to take on the wavy shape shown in the photograph.

Cut the carrot into thin circular slices, and quarter the slices. Boil the carrot pieces for about 2 minutes in a little water with a pinch of salt.

Toss the potatoes, carrot slices, cucumber, and seasonings. Garnish with raisins before serving.

Calories	156
Fat	0.2g
Carbohydrates	38.4g
Fiber	2.3g
Sodium	394mg

SWEET POTATOES AND APPLES

2 medium sweet potatoes
1 apple
2 tablespoons raisins
1 cup water
1 teaspoon salt
juice of 1 lemon
1 tablespoon honey
cinnamon to taste

DIRECTIONS:

Cut the sweet potatoes into thin circular slices. Cut the apple into very thin slices, and then quarter the slices (see photograph). Layer the sweet potatoes, apple pieces, and raisins in a sauce pan, mixing in the salt, lemon juice, honey, and one cup of water.

Japanese cooks use a pan with a small inner lid that sits directly on top of the vegetables. A circle cut out of parchment paper can be substituted for this inner lid. Boil the vegetables with an inner lid and outer lid on the pan until all pieces are soft.

Arrange on a serving dish and sprinkle with cinnamon.

TARO WITH SESAME

2 cups taro
1 tablespoon crushed walnut meats
1 tablespoon sesame cream
2 tablespoons white miso
1 tablespoon mirin
1 tablespoon sake
1 teaspoon salt

GARNISH:
small spring onion as needed
safflower or other edible blossoms as needed

DIRECTIONS:

Steam the whole taro until you can peel the skin off easily. Pound half of the taro meat in a mortar. Mix the pounded taro with coarsely cut walnut bits, sesame cream, white miso, sake, mirin, and salt.

Cut the rest of the taro into bite-sized pieces and add to the taro mixture. Serve in a bowl and sprinkle with chopped spring onion and safflower.

Calories..............178
Fat......................9.5g
Carbohydrates....15.1g
Fiber...................0.8g
Sodium...............591mg

JAPANESE YAM CAKES

2 cups Japanese yam
$^1/_2$ minced onion
2 tablespoons kuzu starch or cornstarch
3 tablespoons whole wheat flour
1 tablespoon sesame seeds
1 teaspoon salt

SAUCE:
3 tablespoons soy sauce
3 tablespoons mirin
aonori

DIRECTIONS:

Grate the unpeeled Japanese yam. Mix the grated yam with the onion, kuzu starch or cornstarch, flour, sesame, and salt. Stir well. Pour the mixture into a shallow dish and bake in a preheated oven at 350 degrees for 10 minutes.

Mix the sauce ingredients and brush the sauce over the baked yam. Sprinkle with aonori and cut it into smaller pieces for serving.

Calories.............154
Fat.....................1.5g
Carbohydrates..28.3g
Fiber..................1.5g
Sodium..............1142mg

Calories...............46
Fat.......................0.1g
Carbohydrates....9.8g
Fiber....................1.8g
Sodium...............787mg

ONION SALAD

2 onions
1 green pepper
2 pickled plums

SAUCE:
3 tablespoons apple vinegar
1 teaspoon honey
1 teaspoon salt

DIRECTIONS:
   Slice the onions and green pepper from side to side into long thin pieces.
Break the pickled plums into pieces.
   Mix the onion and green pepper in a bowl, adding the pickled plums to
the salad. Just before eating, pour the mixed sauce ingredients over the salad.

Calories...............71
Fat.......................0.1g
Carbohydrates....15.1g
Fiber....................2.3g
Sodium...............787mg

PUMPKIN WITH SILVER SAUCE

Japanese pumpkin is much smaller and tastier than its Western cousins.
A small American pumpkin or any small yellow squash can be substituted.

1/2 Japanese pumpkin
3 cups soup stock
2 tablespoons mirin
2 teaspoon salt
2 tablespoons kuzu starch or cornstarch
2 tablespoons water

GARNISH:
shredded ginger as needed

DIRECTIONS:
   Cut the pumpkin into squarish pieces and round off the corners. Place the
pumpkin pieces, with soup stock, mirin, and salt, into a sauce pan and bring
the ingredients to a boil. Once the pumpkin is soft, add kuzu starch dissolved
in water to thicken the soup.
   Serve in a bowl, floating shredded ginger on the top.

PUMPKIN STRINGS

2 cups Japanese pumpkin skin
1 tablespoon egoma oil
$^{1}/_{3}$ cup soup stock
2 tablespoons soy sauce
2 tablespoons mirin
1 tablespoon sake

GARNISH:
roasted white sesame seeds

DIRECTIONS:
   Slice the pumpkin skin into fine strips. Heat the egoma oil in a thick sauce pan and saute the strips in it. Add the soup stock and boil, keeping the pot covered.
   When the pumpkin-skin strips are well cooked, add the soy sauce, sake, and mirin.
   Grind the roasted white sesame seeds and sprinkle them on the pumpkin strings just before serving.

Calories...............57
Fat.......................2.0g
Carbohydrates....7.0g
Fiber....................1.5g
Sodium...............591mg

BOILED PUMPKIN
WITH ADZUKI BEANS

$^1/_4$ Japanese pumpkin
$^1/_2$ cup boiled adzuki beans
soup stock as needed
2 tablespoons mirin
2 tablespoons sake
3 tablespoons light soy sauce

DIRECTIONS:

Cut the pumpkin into 1-inch squares, round off the corners of each piece, and score the skin as in the photograph. Place the squares in a sauce pan, barely covering them with soup stock. Boil and season the pumpkin pieces with sake, mirin, and soy sauce. Add the boiled adzuki beans and continue cooking them until the seasonings are absorbed, about 15 minutes.

Calories..............92
Fat......................0.2g
Carbohydrates....16.2g
Fiber...................2.3g
Sodium...............827mg

Calories...............49
Fat.......................1.9g
Carbohydrates....4.6g
Fiber....................2.7g
Sodium...............354mg

SPINACH SALAD WITH MINCED PINE NUTS

1 bunch spinach
3 tablespoons pine nuts
1 tablespoon mirin
1 1/2 tablespoons light (usukuchi) soy sauce

DIRECTIONS:

Boil the spinach briefly in lightly salted water, then dip it in cold water with a dash of soy sauce to cool. Drain the spinach, squeeze out the excess water, and shred it into bite-size lengths. Add the mirin and soy sauce, and mix well.

Mince the pine nuts on a cutting board and add them to the spinach, tossing well.

Calories...............57
Fat.....................2.2g
Carbohydrates....5.0g
Fiber...................2.7g
Sodium...............551mg

EDIBLE CHRYSANTHEMUM LEAVES DRESSED WITH MUSTARD SESAME

Edible chrysanthemum leaves are called shungiku in Japanese. They can be found at Japanese food stores and other Asian food markets. They have a sharp, refreshing taste and are always served parboiled, boiled, or stewed. Never use garden or hothouse chrysanthemum leaves. You can substitute any savory greem, including endive, mustard greens, broccoli rabe, or radicchio.

---

1 bunch edible chrysanthemum leaves

DRESSING:
2 tablespoons soy sauce
1 tablespoon mirin
1 tablespoon sake
1 teaspoon mustard
2 tablespoons roasted white sesame seeds

DIRECTIONS:

Cook the chrysanthemum leaves in lightly salted boiling water for about 1 minute, drain, and cut into 1-inch lengths.

Pulverize the white sesame seed in a mortar by stirring the pestle in a clockwise direction for about 2 to 3 minutes. The seeds will be partially crushed, but not yet ground into a paste. Add the soy sauce, mirin, and mustard, mixing well until the dressing is smooth.

Toss the leaves in the dressing.

Serve sprinkled with additional ground sesame seeds.

EGGPLANT WITH SESAME MISO SAUCE

Japanese eggplants are much smaller and more tender and tasty than the large Italian eggplants most widely available. Look for the long, slender Japanese eggplants in Asian food stores. Some of the better produce stores have begun to carry them as well in recent years. If you must substitute, pick the smallest ripe Italian eggplants you can find, and probably one will be more than enough.

---

2 small eggplants
2 tablespoons white miso
$1/2$ tablespoon sesame cream
1 tablespoon mirin
1 tablespoon sake

GARNISH:
grated ginger
carrot (julienne)

DIRECTIONS:

Steam the eggplants and peel them. Cut the meat of the eggplants into 1-inch lengths. Boil the shredded carrot in lightly salted water until soft.

Mix the miso, sesame cream, mirin, and sake, and pour the mixture into a bowl. Add the eggplant to the sauce, garnishing with ginger and julienned carrot.

Calories...............67
Fat.......................1.9g
Carbohydrates....8.7g
Fiber....................2.7g
Sodium................197mg

Calories............238
Fat.....................1.9g
Carbohydrates..37.2g
Fiber..................4.3g
Sodium..............2165mg

BAKED EGGPLANT WITH FOUR-COLORED MISO

This dish requires a little extra preparation to create four different colors of miso topping for the eggplant slices, but when assembled with some care and flair, it is as dramatic as it is tasty. This is also one of the few Japanese eggplant recipes in which the larger Italian eggplants work just as well, or even better.

---

2 large eggplants
3 tablespoons hatcho miso
I tablespoon sake
2 tablespoons mirin
8 tablespoons white miso
4 tablespoons sake
4 tablespoons mirin
$1/4$ teaspoon turmeric
I teaspoon aonori

SILVER SAUCE:
2 cups soup stock
2 tablespoons mirin
I tablespoon sake
I teaspoon salt
I tablespoon light soy sauce
I tablespoon kuzu starch
I tablespoon water

GARNISH:
poppy seeds

DIRECTIONS:

Cut the eggplants into circular slices about I-inch thick. Fry them in sesame oil.

Add I tablespoon of sake and 2 tablespoons of mirin to the hatcho miso. Heat the mixture, stirring with a wooden spoon until a smooth paste forms.

Combine 4 tablespoons of sake and 4 tablespoons of mirin with the white miso. Heat this mixture and stir until a smooth paste forms. Divide the white miso into three equal portions.

Add the turmeric to one part of the white miso and stir it until the color changes.

Mix the aonori into the second miso portion, again mixing until it takes on the color of the aonori.

Take the hatcho miso, the remaining white miso, and the two colored misos and spoon over the fried eggplants in circles. Brown in the oven set on broil, being careful not to burn the miso.

Boil the soup stock, adding the seasonings to make the silver sauce. Use the kuzu starch mixed with water to thicken.

Place the eggplant and miso on a large serving plate and pour the sauce gently over it. Sprinkle poppy seeds on top before serving.

GREEN ASPARAGUS DRESSED WITH MUSTARD AND VINEGARED MISO

You can vary this dish by experimenting with different mustards, including Chinese mustard, Japanese wasabi (be careful!), or a sweetened mustard—in which case, cut back on the mirin.

1 bunch fresh green asparagus

DRESSING:
3 tablespoons white miso
1 tablespoon sake
2 tablespoons mirin
2 tablespoons vinegar
mustard powder (or paste) to taste

DIRECTIONS:
Boil the asparagus for about 3 minutes in lightly salted water and cut into bite-size lengths.

Mix the sake, mirin, and mustard powder with the white miso for dressing.

Calories...............69
Fat.....................0.4g
Carbohydrates....11.3g
Fiber...................1.1g
Sodium...............276mg

Calories..............88
Fat.......................6.2g
Carbohydrates....3.2g
Fiber....................1.4g
Sodium...............787mg

GREEN BEANS DRESSED WITH TOFU MAYONNAISE

2 cups green beans

TOFU MAYONNAISE:
1/2 block tofu
3 tablespoons vinegar
1 tablespoon sesame cream
1/4 teaspoon turmeric
2 tablespoons salt
pepper (to taste)

GARNISH:
safflower (or other edible blossom) to taste

DIRECTIONS:
    Boil the green beans in lightly salted water for about 3 minutes.
    Mix the tofu, vinegar, sesame cream, turmeric, salt, and pepper in a blender until smooth to make the tofu mayonnaise. The ingredients can also be pounded in a mortar or whipped quickly in a bowl if a blender is not available.
    Dress the green beans with the mayonnaise and garnish with the safflower.

SNOW PEAS WITH POUNDED SESAME DRESSING

Baby string beans, cut in the French style, are also delicious with this dressing.

1 cup snow peas

DRESSING:
1 tablespoon white sesame seeds
1 tablespoon mirin
1 tablespoon light (usukuchi) soy sauce

DIRECTIONS:
Bring salted water to a boil and add the snow peas. Simmer until tender, then shred the snow peas diagonally.

Parch the white sesame seeds and pound them in a mortar until they are a paste. Mix in the rest of the dressing ingredients until smooth, and pour the dressing over the shredded snow peas.

OKRA BOILED WITH SOUP STOCK

10 okra
soup stock (enough to cover the okra)
2 tablespoons mirin
2 tablespoons sake
1 tablespoon light (usukuchi) soy sauce
1 teaspoon salt

GARNISH:
white sesame seeds

DIRECTIONS:
   Peel off the calyxes of the okra completely. Add sake, mirin, soy sauce, and salt to the soup stock. Boil the okra in the stock for 2 to 3 minutes.
   Serve with sesame seeds sprinkled on top.

Calories..............52
Fat......................0.5g
Carbohydrates....7.8g
Fiber....................2.6g
Sodium...............630mg

STUFFED FRESH SHIITAKE

Fresh shiitake are one of the delights of Japanese cuisine, and baking them, as in this recipe, only intensifies their full, meaty flavor. Finely diced eggplant can be substituted for the gluten burger to vary the recipe, but make sure to dehydrate the eggplant before dicing.

8 fresh shiitake mushrooms

STUFFING:
2/3 cup gluten burger
1 tablespoon kuzu starch or cornstarch
1 teaspoon ginger juice
1 teaspoon sake
1 teaspoon salt
flour as needed

GARNISH:
aonori
lemon wedges

DIRECTIONS:
   Remove the stems from the mushrooms. Wash the mushrooms quickly and drain them. Dust the kuzu starch or cornstarch on the underside of the cap (this will help the stuffing to stick). Stir the stuffing ingredients well, then stuff the mushrooms with it.

   Bake the stuffed mushrooms in a preheated oven at 300 degrees for 7 or 8 minutes. When done, garnish with aonori and serve with lemon wedges.

Calories...............68
Fat......................2.8g
Carbohydrates....8.5g
Fiber...................2.1g
Sodium...............472mg

Calories...............66
Fat.....................2.5g
Carbohydrates....10.6g
Fiber...................2.1g
Sodium...............591mg

SHIITAKE WITH SESAME

8 fresh shiitake mushrooms
sake (to taste)
salt (to taste)
$1/3$ piece fresh ginger (shredded)
2 tablespoons white sesame seeds
2 tablespoons light (usukuchi) soy sauce
2 tablespoons mirin

GARNISH:
8 gingko nuts, boiled in lightly salted water for 5 minutes
kukonomi as needed

DIRECTIONS:

Cut the shiitake mushrooms into small lengths and steam them with sake and salt.

Shred the ginger. Roast the white sesame seeds in a non-stick frying pan.

Grate the sesame and mix it with the light (usukuchi) soy sauce and mirin. Roll the shiitake in the ginger and sesame mixture until the pieces are coated.

Serve decorated with gingko nuts and kukonomi.

OSTRICH FERN DRESSED WITH
VINEGAR MISO SAUCE

Fern fronds are often available in fine food stores in the spring. They have a crunchy texture that is delicious.

---

1 bunch ostrich fern fronds

DRESSING:
3 tablespoons white miso
2 tablespoons mirin
1 tablespoon sake
2 tablespoons vinegar
mustard

GARNISH:
pine nuts as needed

DIRECTIONS:
    Boil the ostrich fern fronds in lightly salted water until tender, drain, and then cut them into 1-inch lengths.

    Mix the dressing ingredients thoroughly.

    Serve the ostrich fern with the vinegar-miso dressing poured on top. Garnish with pine nuts.

Calories...............84
Fat......................1.0g
Carbohydrates....12.8g
Fiber....................3.8g
Sodium...............315mg

Calories..............22
Fat......................0.2g
Carbohydrates....4.1g
Fiber...................0.8g
Sodium...............236mg

PEANUT SALAD

1 cup raw peanuts
2 tablespoons vinegar
1 tablespoon soy sauce

GARNISH:
raisins
sunflower seeds

DIRECTIONS:
   Boil the peanuts in salted water for 20 minutes. Drain them and then mix them in a large bowl with the vinegar and the soy sauce. Sprinkle the raisins and sunflower seeds on top before serving.

WHITE BEAN SALAD

¹/₂ cup boiled white beans
¹/₂ Japanese cucumber

DRESSING:
2 tablespoons vinegar
1 tablespoon honey
1 teaspoon salt

GARNISH:
parsley
kukonomi

DIRECTIONS:
   Grate the cucumber and mix it with the boiled white beans, adding vinegar, honey, and salt. Toss very lightly and serve garnished with minced parsley and kukonomi.

Calories	137
Fat	0.8g
Carbohydrates	23.5g
Fiber	7.0g
Sodium	394mg

Calories............199
Fat....................6.2g
Carbohydrates..17.5g
Fiber.................7.9g
Sodium.............1142mg

SOYBEANS WITH MIXED VEGETABLES

1 cup soy beans
2 cups water
1/2 burdock root
1/2 lotus root
1/2 carrot
1/2 block konnyaku
3 pieces dried shiitake mushroom (reconstituted with water)
soup stock (enough to cover the ingredients)
1/3 cup soy sauce
2 tablespoons sake
3 tablespoons mirin

GARNISH:
cooked green peas

DIRECTIONS:

Place the soy beans in a pressure cooker with 2 cups of water. Cook on high until boiling, then turn down to low heat and cook for an additional 15 minutes.

While the beans are cooking, cube the burdock root, lotus root, carrot, konnyaku, and shiitake. Pour the stock into a different pot and add the cooked soy beans and vegetables. Simmer until tender. Add the soy sauce, sake, and mirin, and simmer again until the beans absorb the flavors, about 10 minutes.

Serve hot with cooked green peas sprinkled on top.

GRILLED TOFU PATTIES WITH SWEET SAUCE

1 firm ("cotton") tofu block
1 medium lotus root
1 medium carrot
3 tablespoons kuzu starch or cornstarch
4 gluten sheets
1 1/2 teaspoons salt
sesame oil as needed

SWEET SAUCE:
2 tablespoons sake
2 tablespoons mirin
2 tablespoons soy sauce
1 tablespoon brown sugar
1/2 tablespoon kuzu starch or cornstarch
1 tablespoon water

GARNISH:
poppy seeds

DIRECTIONS:

Drain the water from the tofu by squeezing it in a dish towel, wringing the cloth with the tofu inside to remove excess moisture. Then mash the tofu in a mortar until smooth.

Finely grate the lotus root and carrot.

Lightly squeeze the grated lotus root and carrot in your hands to extract the juice. Dissolve 3 tablespoons kuzu starch in the juice. In a mixing bowl, add all of the tofu, lotus root, carrot, and salt. Mix thoroughly. Then form 4 equal-sized balls out of the tofu mixture. The dissolved kuzu starch will act as a binding agent to keep the balls together. Set aside.

Sift 1 1/2 tablespoons of kuzu starch and set aside.

Moisten the gluten sheets by patting them with a clean, damp dish towel, then thinly sprinkle the dry kuzu starch over the four sheets. Place one ball of the tofu mixture on one sheet of gluten and flatten the tofu mixture to fully cover the sheet. Repeat until all four sheets are covered. Dust the remaining dry kuzu starch over the squares.

Score the squares with several sharp cuts on the top, and fry them in the sesame oil.

Dissolve 1/2 tablespoon of kuzu starch in one tablespoon of water for the sweet sauce. Set aside.

Mix together all of the sweet sauce ingredients except the kuzu starch in a small pan and bring to a boil. After boiling for a few minutes, add the dissolved kuzu starch to thicken.

Spread the sauce over the fried gluten blocks, cutting them into smaller squares if desired, and garnish them with poppy seeds.

Calories.............183
Fat.....................4.9g
Carbohydrates..23.6g
Fiber..................2.3g
Sodium..............1336 mg

Calories...............173
Fat.....................6.6g
Carbohydrates....17.7g
Fiber..................2.4g
Sodium...............866mg

TOFU WITH MISO CREAM

1 block tofu
1 small carrot
$1/2$ cup green beans
$1/2$ bunch shimeji mushrooms
3 $1/3$ tablespoons flour
1 cup soy milk
4 tablespoons white miso
1 teaspoon salt
sesame oil as needed
dried bread crumbs as needed

DIRECTIONS:

Drain the tofu and cut it into the bite-size pieces. Shred the carrot and boil it briefly in lightly salted water until tender, then set it aside. Boil the green beans in lightly salted water until soft. Drain and cut into 1-inch lengths.

Pour sesame oil into a pan and heat it to fry the shredded carrot and green beans. While frying, add the tofu to the vegetables and stir fry gently, sprinkling salt over the ingredients. Remove the pan from the flame after a few minutes.

Mix flour and soy milk with a wooden spatula until the mixture thickens. Add miso and stir until all ingredients are thoroughly mixed together.

Coat a small casserole dish with sesame oil. Add the tofu, fried vegetables, and shimeji mushrooms and then pour the miso mixture over all. Spread dry bread crumbs across the top and bake the mixture in the oven at 350 degrees until it turns light brown (approximately 10 minutes).

HIJIKI SALAD

$^1/_4$ cup dried hijiki
5 snow peas
$^1/_2$ small carrot
$^1/_2$ cup soup stock
I tablespoon soy sauce
I cup soup stock
$^1/_2$ tablespoon mirin
$^1/_2$ tablespoon soy sauce

DRESSING:
I tablespoon vinegar
I tablespoon light (usukuchi) soy sauce
I teaspoon mirin
I tablespoon pine nuts

GARNISH:
dried yellow chrysanthemum

DIRECTIONS:

Reconstitute the hijiki in water and boil it with $^1/_2$ cup of soup stock and I tablespoon of soy sauce. Drain and set aside.

Boil the snow peas. When soft, drain them and shred them diagonally. Shred the carrot and boil it quickly, removing it from the heat when soft. Drain it. Parboil the yellow chrysanthemum for about 30 seconds with a little vinegar and drain. Shred the shiitake mushroom and boil it in I cup of soup stock, $^1/_2$ tablespoon of mirin, and $^1/_2$ tablespoon of soy sauce.

Mix the hijiki with the vegetables and the yellow chrysanthemum. Dress with the pine nuts, vinegar, light soy sauce, and mirin.

Calories...............32
Fat.......................1.4g
Carbohydrates....6.7g
Fiber...................3.3g
Sodium................763mg

Calories.............159
Fat....................5.4g
Carbohydrates..16.1g
Fiber.................10.4g
Sodium..............2156mg

STEAMED VEGETABLE CASSEROLE

Many delicious Japanese dishes are simmered or steamed over a flame in a large ceramic pan called a nabe. (The pans are available in Japanese supermarkets.) They are usually eaten directly from the pan, each diner selecting pieces with his chopsticks and then dipping them in a sauce. This is a perfect meal for a chilly winter evening.

$^1/_4$ **Chinese cabbage (or any cabbage)**
2 cups bean sprouts
1 bunch edible chrysanthemum leaves
2 long leeks
4 fresh shiitake mushrooms
1 bunch enoki mushrooms
1 bunch shimeji mushrooms
1 block tofu
$^1/_2$ **small carrot**
3 tablespoons sake

DIPPING SAUCE:
4 pieces kabosu soup
8 tablespoons soy sauce
yuzu pepper

DIRECTIONS:

Chop Chinese cabbage into 1-inch lengths. Cut the long leek diagonally. Cut the shiitake mushrooms into decorative shapes. Cut the clump of enoki mushroom in half lengthwise. Disentangle the shimeji mushrooms. Cut the tofu into $^1/_2$-inch cubes. Slice the carrot into small, circular slices and shape into decorative flower or geometric pieces.

Arrange the ingredients in a ceramic baking pan with a lid. Pour sake over the mixture and replace the lid. Steam the vegetables at high heat over a gas or electric burner for 5 to 6 minutes. Turn off the heat and leave the vegetables in the baking pan with the lid closed for another 5 minutes.

Serve with the dipping sauce.

SIMMERED VEGETABLES WITH SAUCE

3 leaves Chinese cabbage (or any other type of cabbage)
1 medium onion
1 medium carrot
3/4 cup bamboo sprouts
1/2 cup fresh peas
4 dried shiitake mushrooms (reconstituted in water)
1 teaspoon egoma oil
1 cup soup stock
1 tablespoon salt
2 tablespoons sake
2 tablespoons kuzu starch
2 tablespoons water

GARNISH:
8 gingko nuts

DIRECTIONS:

Cut the vegetables into bite-size pieces. Dissolve 2 tablespoons of kuzu starch in 2 tablespoons of water and set aside. Heat the egoma oil in the pan and saute the vegetables in order of their hardness. Add soup stock, season with salt and sake, and simmer for about 10 minutes. Thicken the soup with dissolved kuzu starch.

Scatter the gingko nuts over the vegetables before serving.

Calories............100
Fat.....................2.1g
Carbohydrates..18.6 g
Fiber..................5.4g
Sodium.............1501mg

Calories.............319
Fat.....................5.0g
Carbohydrates..57.5g
Fiber.................6.6g
Sodium.............1601mg

CREAM STEW

4 medium potatoes
1 medium carrot
2 medium turnips
2 onions
4 dried shiitake mushrooms (reconstituted with water)
4 cups soup stock
2 tablespoons sake
1 tablespoon salt
pepper
2 cups soy milk
$1/2$ cup flour

GARNISH:
1 chopped spring onion

DIRECTIONS:
Cut the vegetables into large chunky pieces. Cut the shiitake mushrooms into bite-sized pieces.

Add the vegetables and shiitake mushrooms to the soup stock and bring to a boil. Continue boiling until the vegetables grow soft, seasoning with sake, salt, and pepper. Mix the soy milk and flour together, and then add it to thicken the soup.

Season with chopped spring onion and serve hot in a large bowl.

KENCHIN SOUP

1/4 radish
1/2 medium carrot
1/2 burdock
1/2 pack shimeji mushrooms
1 block tofu
1 bunch edible chrysanthemum leaves
12 gingko nuts
6 cups soup stock
3 tablespoons sake
2 tablespoons mirin
1 teaspoon salt
4 tablespoons light (usukuchi) soy sauce

DIRECTIONS:

Slice the radishes and carrots into thin, circular slices. Quarter each slice. Grate the burdock root using the coarsest blade of a grater, making thin strings of the root. Put the radishes, carrots, and grated burdock in the soup stock and boil the vegetables until they are soft.

Cut the tofu into 1/4-inch squares and add to the soup. The tofu can also be crumbled by hand before adding, depending on how you want it to look.

Season the soup with sake, mirin, salt, and soy sauce. Bring the soup to a boil again and then turn down the heat. Cut the edible chrysanthemum leaves into 1-inch lengths and boil them in the soup.

Float the gingko nuts in the soup and serve hot in a large serving bowl.

Calories............171
Fat....................4.2g
Carbohydrates..18.1g
Fiber..................4.9g
Sodium..............1192mg

The "weathermark" identifies this book as a production of Weatherhill, Inc., publishers of fine books on Asia and the Pacific. Editorial supervision: Jeffrey Hunter. Book and cover design: Mariana Canelo. Production supervision: Bill Rose. Printed and bound by Oceanic Graphic Printing, Hong Kong. The typeface used is Gill Sans.